Last Minute Meetings

By Fern Dickey, CMP

CAREER
PRESS

Franklin Lakes, NJ

Last Minute Meetings

Cover design by Foster & Foster
Printed in the U.S.A. by Book-mart Press

To order this title, please call toll-free 1-800-CAREER-1 (NJ and Canada: 201-848-0310) to order using VISA or MasterCard, or for information on books from Career Press.

The Career Press, Inc., 3 Tice Road, PO Box 687,
Franklin Lakes, NJ 07417

www.careerpress.com

Library of Congress Cataloging-in-Publication Data

Dickey, Fern.
  Last minute meetings / by Fern Dickey
    p. cm.
  Includes index.
  ISBN 1-56414-497-6 (paper)
    1. Business meetings. I. Title.
HF5734.5 .D53 2000   00-050711

Dedication and Acknowledgments

With my love, to my husband Bill.

Many thanks to Bob Bly, for generously offering his expertise, advice, and support; to my Mom and to Mom and Dad Dickey for their love and encouragement; and to my friend Suzanne Updegraff, who introduced me to meeting planning.

Contents

Introduction 7

Chapter 1: Last Minute Meeting Planning 9

Chapter 2: Last Minute Budget Creation 23

Chapter 3: Last Minute Site Selection 39

Chapter 4: Last Minute Promotions 51

Chapter 5: Finding Speakers 65

Chapter 6: Working with the Facility 83

Chapter 7: Communicating with Attendees 99

Chapter 8: Working with Vendors 113

Chapter 9: Legal Issues 129

Chapter 10: Miscellaneous Meeting Particulars 143

Chapter 11: The Big Event 153

Appendix 167

Glossary of Meeting Terms 175

Index 189

Introduction

There are lots of last minute projects that are thrown to people to complete — on time, on schedule, and on budget. The nature of event planning doesn't lend itself to "last minute." The project management of an event is administering detail after detail. And once you've announced or promoted your meeting date, very rarely can you change it to give yourself more planning time.

But last minute meetings happen and can be planned successfully. It helps if a professional meeting planner can give you sample forms and letters, tips, planning steps, and other resources. This way, you don't have to re-create or search for them. *Last Minute Meetings* comes to the rescue, so that you can use your time efficiently.

I wrote this book with two things in mind: You don't have much time, and this is all new to you. I think you'll find it easy to read and easy to follow. Here we go.

Chapter 1

Last Minute Meeting Planning

"A program plan is the flight plan for the meeting experience."

— *Professional Meeting Management, 3rd Edition*

U nlike lots of other projects, it's usually impossible to reschedule a meeting or get an extension. Your colleague may get an extra few days to write that brochure or take another week to get her strategic plan in to the boss, but for your meeting the date is the date. Ready or not, the meeting is going to take place. Can you pull it all together at the last minute?

To plan the perfect meeting, you need to be efficient. What does "being efficient" mean? In terms of planning, you've got to make a list of *every* detail. Give each detail a deadline and assign it to a team or person. Meet frequently with the people who are helping you plan—depending on how much there is to do and how soon your meeting is taking place, you may want to meet for a few minutes each day to review your list.

Program planning

Meeting purpose

To ensure the success of your meeting, give the meeting a *raison d'etre* — a reason for living. Here are the things you (and others) will need to agree upon to develop and solidify your program. Everything you do after this initial planning is done simply to support the program.

Note: Any type of history is invaluable in planning future programs. The history can tell you about how the program has been structured in the past, whether it has been successful (via evaluations), destinations, the kind of space that was needed (for example, did you need 3,000 square feet for a vendor area in addition to regular meeting space for 100 attendees), dates, number of attendees, budgets, past speakers and topics, and what purposes/objectives the program served (for example, networking, continuing education credits, board/member meeting).

Objectives

There are always two sets of objectives: one for your organization and one for the attendees. The objectives must be quantifiable. Otherwise, how do you know they've been met?

Your organization's goals will likely revolve around meeting a certain number. (For example, "the X association's e-commerce symposium will attract 200 attendees each paying $300, for a registration income of $60,000"). The goals for the attendees will have to do with their participation (for example, "95 percent of the evaluations will indicate that the educational sessions exceeded their expectations").

Title, theme, and content

Having a theme and title for your program helps keep you focused. It also makes it a lot easier to select session topics, write and design promotions, and generate interest in your event. Often your theme becomes your marketing tagline. Here are some examples that have come across my desk recently: Web Design World: Publishing for the New Millennium; Innovative Thinking Conference #10: Inventing Tomorrow; and DMDNY's 35th Annual Marketing Conference & Exposition: Direct Marketing...The Key to E-commerce Success.

Research

There are many easy ways to quickly understand the timely and important topics your attendees need.

The first easy method is to review four or five recent issues of several trade magazines, newspapers, and newsletters. Go through them in search of common themes, important news, and interesting features.

Secondly, interview and survey people who represent your audience. Conduct phone interviews and mail surveys. Phone interviews can be quick and casual; 10 minutes per call is probably enough time. Be selective about who you call, and just ask a couple of open-ended questions. Questions that get the ball rolling include, "What challenges at work keep you up at night? What keeps your employees (or colleagues) up at night? What is the biggest challenge you are facing today?" Short one-page surveys mailed or faxed to either past attendees or prospective attendees provide an clear understanding of the audience's needs.

Another especially good method for planning is to work with an appointed education committee. For example, contact 10–15 industry people your organization respects and trusts and invite them to participate as committee members. During your planning process you'll meet with these people (usually via phone conference) to review your meeting's theme, content, and topics. They help you make sure you're on track with selecting appropriate sessions.

The best results will come from using all of these methods to get an overall "big picture."

Format

Decide on the length of your program and how many hours will be allotted for meetings and education as well as social functions and free time.

The two typical program formats are the general session (where all attendees are in one room) and the breakout sessions (smaller groups where specific topics are discussed, usually with two or three simultaneous breakouts to give attendees a choice of topic). However, planning a three-day meeting of just general and breakout sessions will be boring! Mix it up with different kinds of presentations: panel sessions with a moderator, roundtables, hands-on sessions, and using audience-response systems (that is, equipment that allows the audience to electronically submit their responses, which are then automatically tabulated and projected onto a screen). Also, if you are at a wonderful destination, take advantage of what the location offers — whether that means getting a meeting room with a view or using the property's gardens and pools.

Lay out your program in a grid. It makes it easy to review, you can see at a glance if there are time conflicts, and it will give you a sense of the flow of the event. See Figure 1.1 for a sample program schedule.

Figure 1.1

Annual Widget Conference
Registry Resort, Naples, FL
(as of June 28)

TUESDAY, FEBRUARY 16

TIME	SESSION TYPE
1:30–4:30 p.m.	Executive Committee Meeting (12 people)

WEDNESDAY, FEBRUARY 17

TIME	SESSION TYPE
12:00–5:15 p.m.	Board Lunch/Meeting (30 to 45 people)
5:15–6:00 p.m.	First-Timers' Reception (100 people)
6:00–7:00 p.m.	Chairman's Welcome Reception (190+ people)

THURSDAY, FEBRUARY 18

TIME	SESSION TYPE
7:30–8:30 a.m.	BREAKFAST MEETING sponsored by program sponsors (120 people)
8:30–8:45 a.m.	Refreshment Break (100 people)
8:45 a.m.–noon	GENERAL SESSION (200 people)
1:00–5:00 p.m.	Golf Tournament (135 people)
1:30–3:00 p.m.	(4) CONCURRENT BREAKOUT SESSIONS (20–60 per room)
7:00–10:00 p.m.	Theme Party (225 people)

FRIDAY, FEBRUARY 19

TIME	SESSION TYPE
7:00–8:30 a.m.	(4) CONCURRENT BREAKFAST BREAKOUT SESSIONS (20–60 people per room)
8:30–8:45 a.m.	Refreshment Break (120 people)
8:45 a.m.–noon	GENERAL SESSION (200 people)
1:30–4:30 p.m.	Tennis Tournament (35 people)
1:30–3:30 p.m.	GENERAL SESSION (200 people)
Evening	Dine-Around
9:00–11:00 p.m.	Dessert reception (200 flow)

SATURDAY, FEBRUARY 20

TIME	SESSION TYPE
7:00–8:30 a.m.	(4) CONCURRENT BREAKFAST BREAKOUT SESSIONS (20–60 people per room)
8:30–8:45 a.m.	Break
8:45–11:15 a.m.	GENERAL SESSION (200 people)
12:30–2:00 p.m.	LUNCHEON NETWORKING/ GENERAL SESSION (120 people)
6:00–7:00 p.m.	Cocktail Reception (230 people)
7:00–10:00 p.m.	Banquet (230 people)

END OF CONFERENCE

Budget

Information concerning your budget and revenue goals should be included in your objectives. Some meetings are expected to break even, while others need to make a profit. Sometimes meetings are even budgeted at a loss. (See Chapter 2 for some tips for creating budgets that work.) For now, have a financial goal in mind as you create the program format. If you need to break even, and your meeting relies solely on the $25 registration fee from an expected audience of 40 people, you won't be able to hire Tom Peters to speak. Nor will you be able to put on a sumptuous buffet lunch or hold an elaborate theme party.

Destination

Your site needs to match your meeting, as does the size of the facility. You wouldn't hold a half-day board meeting in the Florida Keys unless you and your board members reside there. A fundraising banquet for 3,000 couldn't be held at the local Kiwanis Club. Meetings involving people traveling from all over the country are best held at airport hotels or destinations within driving distance of a major airport; meetings for local folks do well at suburban locations. With destination selection, logic prevails.

Speakers

Once you've chosen your topics and decided on the formats for each session, speaker selection begins. Sometimes you will work backwards — that is, you'll choose a speaker and then discuss and select his or her topics. Otherwise you'll be choosing topics and then searching for presenters. Your choices should be based on their knowledge of a topic, their skill as a presenter, their reputation, and, of course, their availability and fee schedule.

Organizing your time

Action plans, timelines, and to do lists

When I'm planning a meeting, I keep two lists. One is a marketing schedule that helps me make sure all the promotions are being created and mailed on time. The other is an action plan—a list of every little detail, from audiovisual requirements for speakers to making sure thank you notes are sent to all the appropriate people. Keeping too many lists will confuse you. Stick to one or two to keep your sanity.

There are parts of two sample action plans here. Figure 1.2 is a month-by-month to-do list for a workshop. Figure 1.3 is part of an "action plan" for an awards banquet. Complete action plans would have steps for each month with a lot more details, but space doesn't permit us to reproduce an entire action plan here. If you keep in mind that the basic steps to planning remain the same, though, it won't be hard to create your own. (A sample marketing plan is included in Chapter 4.)

Simply work backwards from the date of the event to schedule deadlines. Creating the plan in an Excel spreadsheet or in a Word document makes it easy to add details as you learn about them or think about them.

Action plans become an invaluable tool for recurring meetings. As you amass different action plans, you can use them as generic outlines for new kinds of meetings.

Figure 1.2

The Widget Show
June 16-18
[Action Plan]

Month/Task	Assigned To	Due Date	Completed
January			
Submit list of "tried & true" speakers to Seminar Coordinator	FD	1/15	Yes
Coordinator invoices: tracking & splitting cost, discuss w/DKI	TR	1/23	Yes
Let JT @ THE SHOW MGMT. CO. know price & that THE SHOW MGMT. CO. is responsible for registration.	TR/DK	1/24	Yes
Follow up with Seminar Coordinator	TR	ongoing	Yes
Follow up with Partners/deadlines	TR	ongoing	
February			
Develop sponsorship	TR & FD	2/10	
Finalize track titles	Partners/	2/7	Yes
Delineate speaker guidelines	Widget, Inc.	2/7	Yes
	& Widget		
	Assoc.	2/7	Yes
Follow up with Seminar Coordinator	TR	ongoing	
Follow up with Partners/deadlines	TR	ongoing	
March			
Once general sessions confirmed, solicit sponsorships	SU	3/3	
Follow up with Seminar Coordinator	TR	ongoing	
Follow up with Partners/deadlines	TR	ongoing	

Figure 1.3

October 18th Awards Dinner
[Action Plan]

ACTION ITEM	DUE DATE	RESPONSIBILITY	✓	COMMENTS
2000 Site Selection		FD	✓	Review sites in June 1999
2001 Site Selection		FD	✓	Review sites in June 1999
Draft budget		FD	✓	

May/June

ACTION ITEM	DUE DATE	RESPONSIBILITY	✓	COMMENTS
Meet to discuss event: RL, KH, FD, GH, DL, LW		All		
Edit/redesign Award invitation		FD	✓	
Secure donation for invitation		GH		
Call for Nominations		KH	✓	
Call technician to do presentation		FD	✓	
Letter to Award Advisory Committee		RL	✓	
Award recipient advisement		RL		
Invitations addressed, stuffed, mailed		KH		
Order booklet covers, if necessary		KH		

Order medallions, if necessary		SR	✓	Enough in-house
Nomination forms due back		KH	✓	
Brochure specs and donation		DL		
Outgoing Chair Process		FD/RL		See last year's files

September/October

ACTION ITEM	DUE DATE	RESPONSIBILITY	✓	COMMENTS
Order roses for Award spouse		SR		From 4 Seasons
Confirmation letter to band: parking, meals, equipment storage		RW		
Script for evening		FD		
Final guarantee to Signature Room		FD		Order dinner for band
Prepare vendor list for Fern		RW		
Shipping to Four Seasons (Award Material)		GH		For FD: include baggies, 300 paper clips and boxes for badges.
Certificates calligraphied and framed for inductees		SR		
Review/hand out on-site instructions for staff		FD		
Create on-site bible		GH		

ON SITE

Work on reserved table assignments		FD		
Attach meal tickets to name badges		FD/FD		
Walk through of Signature Room				
Drop off plaques to Signature Room				
Staff members to direct guests				
Alert cab companies				

POST

Thank-you letters				
Letters to inductees with extra brochures				
Review 2000 contract				

NOTES:

Shipping includes:

–award medallions

–plaques for award winners

–name badges, badge holders

–ribbons

FOR NEXT YEAR:

–reorder certificates

Managing the details

The meeting planning process has three segments: pre-meeting, on site, and post-meeting. Some of the tasks will be done by you, some by your assistants and colleagues, some by other people and teams within your organization, and some by outside vendors and committees. Your action plan will capture all the details of this process. Depending on the size and type of your meeting, you'll need to review the plan daily or weekly with the people involved so that you always know exactly where you stand.

Delegating

Depending on your organization, other people and organizations will be handling pieces of the program because it's their job or because you hired them to do so. Some meeting planning tasks are very time-consuming. These include registration, finding available meeting space, keeping track of information due from speakers, keeping vendors on track, and certain production tasks (such as coordinating the printing and mailing of promotional pieces). Try to recruit people to help you if it looks like you're expected to do it all yourself. Hiring temporary help is recommended. (See Chapter 8.)

Keeping it stress-free

If you're good about meeting regularly to review your action plan, and if you really follow the plan and help others do the same, your experience should be free from unnecessary stress, if not entirely stress-free. Meeting planning can be broken down into a very mechanical process with standard procedures and steps.

Conclusion

Quick steps

1. Establish the purpose and objectives of the program.
2. Research and choose a program title, theme, topics, and destination.
3. Create the program format.
4. Create (and maintain) an action plan.
5. Keep in constant contact with others in the production process.

Quick tips

🕐 Make the format of your event fresh, fun, and exciting. Think of yourself sitting in the audience — do you want to suffer through each session or learn and have fun?

🕐 Frequent meetings with your planning team help keep you on track and ensure that details are taken care of.

Chapter 2

Last Minute Budget Creation

"What's a thousand dollars? Mere chicken feed. A poultry matter."
—Groucho Marx

E
ven if you're rushing like mad to get your event produced, you must have a budget. It is as important and necessary (maybe even more so) than your action plan. It will certainly be a main criterion determining if your event met its corporate objectives. You'll use your budget to help you make decisions, establish priorities, and keep you on target with meeting expenditures.

Think of your budget as a tool to keep you on track throughout your coordination of the event. You need to know how much money is anticipated to come in, how much you're planning to spend, and the spending limits you need to set so that you're financially secure and you don't end up in a financial quagmire.

Creating quick budgets

If you've never written a budget before, you should ask for some assistance to help you through the process (perhaps your CFO or a colleague). If possible, review budgets from previous events. If this is the first time an event is being held, you will have to make some difficult judgements, such as how many people will attend and your anticipated daily room pick up. (See Chapter 9.)

There are two sections to every budget: income and expenses.

Income

Line items that account for income include:

- Registration fees (usually member and non-member rates).
- Sponsorships.
- Sales of publications, tapes, and any other materials.
- A la carte choices and special events (such as pre-conference workshops or spouse/guest programs).
- Exhibitors (booth or table) sales.

When forecasting income, be conservative. Although I might be confident that I can bring in 100 attendees, I will only budget to bring in approximately 80 percent of that number. Eighty percent is my worst case scenario to prevent my budget coming in lower than anyone's expectations.

Expenses

Expense line items are more extensive. Here's a list of broad expense topics, each with its own set of line items:

- ☺ Travel and lodging for you and other staff members who will be on site.
- ☺ Speaker fees and travel expenses.
- ☺ Vendor expenses (for example, band, florist, photographer, shuttle service).
- ☺ Awards (trophies, certificates, scholarships).
- ☺ Printing and promotion (promotional materials like brochures, handouts, fliers).
- ☺ Facilities expenses (food and beverage, audiovisual, meeting rooms, gratuities).
- ☺ Miscellaneous (program development expenses, conference calls, shipping, badges, ribbons, signage, credit card bank fees, temporary help).
- ☺ Co-sponsor costs (if you are hosting the program with another group).

Breakeven analysis

To determine how many attendees must register, at your proposed registration fee, use *a breakeven/unit* formula:

$$\frac{\text{total fixed expenses}}{(\text{price - variable cost per person})}$$

Fixed expenses are those that aren't going to change, such as speaker fees, meeting room rentals, and photographer and audiovisual charges. Variable expenses vary depending on how many people attend and include the cost of food and beverage, registration kits, and handout materials.

Here's a simple example. Say your registration fee is $250, your total fixed expenses amount to $4,000, and your variable expenses are $35 per person. Your formula would look like this:

$$\frac{\$4{,}000}{(\$250\text{-}\$35)}$$

This calculates to 19 units. In other words, you need 19 registrations to break even.

A *breakeven price analysis* is used to determine what your registration fee should be. The formula is:

$$\frac{\text{total fixed expenses}}{\text{number of attendees}} \;+\; \text{variable expenses}$$

Say your fixed expenses total $20,000; 450 attendees are expected; and variable expenses are projected at $250 per person. This calculates to a *breakeven* registration fee of $295. You need to raise the fee according to the percentage of profit you must make.

There are times, especially when planning a new program, that the breakeven price analysis helps a group decide that a program won't be financially viable and the project is halted or revamped.

Creating a budget sheet

Simple budget sheets have three columns for each line item: the budgeted amount, the actual amount, and the variance. Figure 2.1 is a sample budget for a conference with 400 attendees, three keynote speakers, and 22 breakout sessions held over a two-and-a-half-day period.

Figure 2.1

1999 Widget Conference
Co-sponsored by Widget International
and Widget-Makers, Inc.
May 17–19
Chicago, IL

	Budget	Actual	Variance
REVENUE			
Attendee Revenue:			
Members	$69,500.00	$81,550.00	$12,050.00
Nonmembers	$18,250.00	$9,505.00	-$8,745.00
Pre-conference Workshop Attendees	$15,250.00	$25,570.00	$10,320.00
Sponsor Revenue:			$0.00
Sponsored Events	$19,980.00	$19,585.00	-$395.00
Sponsor Tabletop Exhibits	$79,800.00	$92,270.00	$12,470.00
Gross Revenues	$202,780.00	$228,480.00	$25,700.00
EXPENSES			
Promotion			
Advertising/Press Releases	$2,200.00	$1,290.00	-$910.00
Broadcast Fax Campaign	$200.00	$85.00	-$115.00
Conference Brochure: design/print	$16,000.00	$12,595.00	-3,405.00
Postcard: design/print	$3,000.00	$800.00	-$2,200.00
Brochure: postage/mailing	$18,000.00	$14,100.00	-$3,900.00
Postcard: postage/mailing	$9,000.00	$2,052.00	-$9,948.00
Conference Booklets and Handouts	$3,000.00	$3,376.00	$376.00
Mailing List: purchase	$1,000.00	$1,293.00	$293.00

Awards Banquet (without hotel expenses)

Scholarship Fund	$1,000.00	$500.00	-$500.00
Program/Postage Costs	$3,000.00	$1,418.00	-$1,582.00
Widget Maker of the Year Award	$1,000.00	$950.00	-$50.00
Widget Maker of the Year Brochures	$1,600.00	$995.00	$605.00

Conference Expenses

Speaker Fees	$6,000.00	$3,500.00	-$2,500.00
Speaker Expenses	$7,500.00	$6,500.00	-$1,000.00
Program Development Meetings	$1,500.00	$1,690.00	$190.00
Education Committee	$100.00	$120.00	$20.00
Shipping	$1,000.00	$450.00	-$550.00
Conference Calls	$500.00	$225.00	-$275.00
Photographer	$800.00	$775.00	-$25.00
Signs, Ribbons, Badges	$1,200.00	$885.00	$315.00
Misc. Meeting Materials	$300.00	$95.00	-$205.00
Staff Travel	$2,000.00	$3,200.00	$1,200.00
Credit Card Bank Fees	$2,000.00	$2,661.00	$661.00
Misc.	$700.00	$118.00	-$582.00
Expenses other than hotel	$82,600.00	$59,673.00	- $22,927.00

Hotel

Lodging-Rooms (speakers/ staff)	$6,000.00	$10,800.00	$4,800.00
Food and Beverage	$44,600.00	$45,448.00	$848.00
A/V	$9,000.00	$7,320.00	-$1,680.00
Meeting Rooms	$1,500.00	$1,030.00	-$470.00
Gratuities/Misc.	$2,000.00	$950.00	-$1,050.00
Total Hotel-related Expenses	$63,100.00	$65,548.00	$2,447.00
Total Expenses	$145,700.00	$125,221.00	-$20,479.00
NET	$57,080.00	$103,259.00	$46,179.00

Estimating costs for "The Big Three"

The high cost items will be your hotel expenses (especially food and beverage and audiovisual), speaker fees and expenses, and promotion costs. Let's look at each of the three to see how to plan a budget for each, while still working within your constraints.

Facilities costs. To understand your facilities costs, you need to ask a couple of the venues you're considering to fax you their menus and audiovisual equipment rental list. They'll send you menus for every conceivable function: breakfasts, breaks, lunches, receptions, dinners, and special events (such as setting up a bar in a presidential or hospitality suite). You'll use those menus to figure your costs for each function. Make a chart and list every possible meal event. See Figure 2.2 for an example of a chart created to budget food and beverage expenses. This example accounts for one day of a four-day annual conference for 300 attendees. (Note that taxes and gratuities were added to the figures.)

Figure 2.2

EVENT	COUNT	COST PER PERSON (includes tax/grats)	TOTAL
Monday			
Continental Breakfast	100	$15	$1,450
Coffee Break	135	$6	$810
Spouse/Guest Breakfast	40	$21	$840
Golf Box Lunch	75	$23	$1,725
General Session Luncheon	70	$25	$1,750
Theme Party Reception	215	$11	$2,365
Theme Party Food/Bev. only	215	$60	$12,900
Dinner for band (vendor)	5	$22	$110

Remember to add the cost of the venue's rates for service tax and gratuities.This amount will be somewhere in
28-percent range of your total food and beverage bill.

Estimating head counts

How many people will attend each meal function?
Unless your meeting has a long history and the staff has
been good about record keeping, estimating out how many
people will attend each meal function is one of the hardest
things you'll have to figure out. For more cost-intensive food
functions, such as a banquet, you'll control the "meal count"
by doing two things: (1) asking people to respond if they
are attending via a check box on the registration form (or
returning an RSVP card) and (2) confirming on site by
distributing tickets in each attendee's registration packet and
having them return the ticket to you if they are planning to
attend. Your goal is to give the hotel as accurate a count as
possible so you avoid paying for uneaten meals. If you
miscount by 25 people, and the banquet dinners cost $22 per
person, plus tax and gratuity, you've misspent $700 dollars.

Otherwise, figure the percentages that you think will
attend each function. Ask a meeting planner or call the two
big meeting planning trade associations, Meeting Professionals International (MPI) or the Professional Convention
Management Association (PCMA) for help with these
percentages.

Controlling speaker expenses. Unless you are absolutely
clear in your letter of agreement with your speaker, you
could end up paying hundreds — or even thousands — of
unexpected dollars.

One of the deadliest budget killers is airfare. Airfares
vary wildly depending on how far in advance the ticket is
booked. Whether or not the speaker is willing to extend his
trip into a Saturday night stayover or travel nonstop instead

of connecting are other considerations. Not purchasing tickets at least 21 days in advance can double or triple the price.

Incur that kind of expense with five or six speakers, and you could spend a few thousand unanticipated dollars. If you have the time and staff, you may want to make the travel arrangements. Otherwise, be crystal clear in your letter of agreement what you will or won't pay for. Some associations give speakers a travel budget and the speakers can use it as they wish — either flying economically on your dollar or using your budget to travel as they wish.

Also, make sure you're very clear about which expenses you will pay and which expenses are the speaker's responsibility. Put language in your contract that covers all the bases: dry cleaning/laundry, golf games, massages, meals, room service, in-room movies, telephone use (have speakers use a calling card), and the expenses of the speaker's guest.

Audiovisual equipment can be another expense albatross. I've worked with some difficult speakers who made last minute on-site requests costing us thousands of dollars. These requests included copying a 30-page handout for 200 attendees (6,000 pages copied at the hotel's business center for 20 cents per page costs $1,200), and an order for an LCD panel and computer cost us $1,500. From these experiences I've learned to create contract elements that set clear limits regarding budgets and last minute, or unreasonable, requests.

Promotions. My advice on the best way to save money here is simple. Here are some tips.

1. Plan carefully and follow your schedule so that you don't have to do last minute promotions, which will incur rush charges and extra postage.

2. Use care in selecting your mailing lists. They're a critical element. Seek advice from marketing experts if possible.

3. Use cost-effective formats. For example, self-mailers will be less expensive than envelope packages.

4. Keep it simple. Don't overdesign or overprint. Use simple two-color pieces as opposed to more expensive four-color. Use clip art rather than expensive stock photography when possible.

Managing the budget

Bids and written agreements

Before you purchase anything from an outside vendor make sure you review a written estimate or contract and sign off on it. You can't control your budget if you don't do this. If you or the vendor make any changes to the original order, put the request and the cost in writing and have both parties sign off on it. A keynote speaker we worked with said he was going to be able to split the cost of his airfare between our group and another group he was going to present to the following day. When we got his invoice, the entire airfare was charged to our group. We didn't have it in writing and he wouldn't return our calls. We ended up paying for the airfare.

When you're reviewing your written agreement, make sure the hotel has listed *all* its costs, including the tax and gratuities charges added to all food functions (upwards of 28 percent the cost) as well as charges for room setups, labor and labor minimums, charges for bartenders and carvers at buffet stations, and so on. Ask the hotel for a Service Information Guide, which will list any of its standard charges that may or may not be in your contract. These can be negotiated. For example, you might ask them to waive room set up charges (see Chapter 9).

Working with your accounting department

The staff of your accounting/finance department are the experts. With their help you can learn to create and manage budgets within the guidelines of your organization's policies and expectations.

You probably already have your own budget sheets made in accordance with your finance department. If not, ask for samples. Use this format to create your meeting budget. That way, when you review the budget with your finance staff, they'll be able to quickly understand it.

Keep your backup notes as well as copies of the separate sheets you've created for each line item, such as the food/beverage cost estimate sheet (see Figure 2.2).

Teamwork

Get everyone in your department involved. Show them the budget you're creating and explain it. Ask for their input on line items that are under their area of expertise or experience. Review the budget with your team on a biweekly basis. Get their suggestions and ideas. When everyone feels like they are a part of the process, they'll do their best to hold to the expenses and perhaps even look for ways to increase the income.

Policies and procedures

Setting standards helps control expenses and helps everyone understand how their requests affect the overall budget.

The first standard to determine is how many free and reduced-fee registrations you can grant. There are always VIPs who are given complimentary passes to an event or people who are granted great discounts for one reason or another. Often, press people are invited to attend events gratis because your company wants the publicity. These free and discounted registrations will cause problems if they aren't budgeted for — especially if the variable expenses for your event are on the high-end. Find out in advance from your company or organization's executives if they are planning to invite guests so you can budget for it.

Cancellation policies must be set and included on both the registration form and attendee confirmations. You may need two cancellation policies: one for the event and one for extracurricular activities that are paid for à la carte. If people can cancel for the à la carte events on site, you'll get stuck paying for their expected attendance. Here's a standard cancellation paragraph:

> Cancellations received on or before [DATE] entitle you to a full refund. Cancellations received after [DATE] will be assessed a $200 administrative charge. You may substitute colleagues from the same company at no additional charge. *Cancellations must be made in writing.* No shows, without written or faxed notice prior to the conference, are responsible for payment in full.

All special and à la carte events must also have a clear cancellation policy. List the policy in the brochure and again on the attendees' registration confirmation if they've signed up for any special events.

On-site budget management

Steady communication with the hotel staff will keep surprises at a minimum. And you must have language in the contract with the hotel stating that you (and others at your discretion) are the only individual authorized to sign for charges related to your organization's function. Try to limit this authorization to one or two key people; it's even better if you are the only one who can sign for expenses. This way, there are no surprises when your final bill arrives.

Review and sign every hotel charge at the end of each day. Check the bills against your banquet event orders (see Chapter 6) to ensure that there aren't any mistakes or changes on pricing, amounts, or charges that don't belong to your group. It's easier to fix potential problems while you're on site than it is when you're home after the event.

There are lots of things that can happen on site to wreak havoc to your budget. You control most of them by being the only person authorized to sign off on charges. But here are a few of the major budget-busters.

The venue's business center can be a lifesaver if you don't have time to run to a local Kinko's or Sir Speedy. However, as I mentioned earlier, hotel business centers often charge a premium for copies, faxing, and other services. Here are some average prices for services:

- ☺ Outgoing faxes: $5 for the first page, $2 for each additional page.
- ☺ Copies: 20 cents per page.
- ☺ Typing services: $10 per page.
- ☺ Transparencies: $2 each.

Your keynote speaker decides he'd like the room set changed from a theatre to a classroom. That's nice, but last minute changes in room setups, unless specified in your contract, will cost you in labor and other charges. For instance, assume a hotel charges $2 per chair plus $25/hour per person for labor with a four-hour minimum. If your general session was set for 300 people, it will cost you $600 for the chairs and at least $200 for the labor (plus tax, of course). This amounts to an unexpected $800. The extra expenses seem trivial, but they add up quickly and can result in a final bill much higher than what you planned for.

Many times, executives will decide to host a meal for sponsors, VIPs, press people, etc. at the last minute. In these instances, unfortunately, there's not much you can do.

Post-event

If you've maintained your budget, it won't be hard to reconcile the final invoices and budget when you're back at the office. The best advice I cna provide, though, is to take the time to carefully review everything. Check speaker and vendor invoices against contracts. Review the facilities bill against your signed on-site paperwork. There are plenty of times when you'll need to correct a hotel bill or remind a speaker, for example, that he signed an agreement stating that your organization wouldn't reimburse speakers for copies of handouts made on site. Here's a sample of a simple letter to a hotel asking for corrections to be made to their final bill:

March 15, 1999
FAX:
Any Hotel
1234 Main Street
Any City, US 12345
ATTN: Group Accounts
RE: [ACCOUNT NUMBER]

We have received the invoice and summary of charges for 1999 Widget Conference held at your hotel February 14–21, 1999. The bill has been reviewed and is with our executive staff for approval before it goes to accounting. I appreciate the clarity of the bill. I only have two adjustments, listed below along with the reasons for the adjustment:

1. Room and Tax. Total deducted: $1,859.00
Per our contract, we are allowed 54 sleeping room nights at the $210 rate. We had only been credited for 28 nights. The deduction covers the difference between the $275 room charge and the $210 room charge for 26 additional room nights. This amount includes the reduction in room tax as well.

2. Food and Beverage. Total deducted: $1,518.94

The final charge for BEO #25874 should be $2,790.00 instead of $4308.94. The price per person was listed as $13.75 with taxes and service charge for a total of $18.36 per person. The guarantee was 152 people for an amount due of $2,790.00. A copy of the BEO follows.

The total amount that should be credited to our bill is **$3,377.94.** Our accounting department will be sending a check for **$85,548.87**. Please call me if you have questions.

Sincerely,

Fern Dickey

Manager, Widget Education

Conclusion

Quick steps

1. Use real numbers to create your budget by doing research and getting written estimates and contracts.
2. Ask for assistance from your finance department and from colleagues.
3. Monitor your budget weekly to make sure you're on track with your projected income and expenses.
4. Monitor your budget on site by reviewing bills daily.
5. Double-check final invoices against your records and contracts before signing off.

Quick tips

- Work closely with your finance department.
- Plan carefully to avoid budget-busters such as on-site photocopies and extra food.

Chapter 3

Last Minute Site Selection

When you're pulling together a meeting at the last minute, finding a place to hold your meeting will likely be your toughest challenge. Depending on the size of the meeting, you'll run into a number of obstacles. If your meeting is small (less than 50 attendees), hotels don't want to waste precious revenue-generating meeting space on you. Conversely, if they do take your meeting, they'll probably charge you an arm and a leg for the meeting room; expect to pay anywhere from $500 to $1,500. If your meeting is large (50 or more people), you'll have trouble finding meeting space and/or sleeping rooms that aren't already booked. Here are some quick tips to find space for your meeting.

People and places who can help

My previous boss gave me a very simple but very powerful piece of advice that has served me well during all my years as a meeting planner: "Ask people for help. People love to be asked." I'll pass that advice on to you. Ask. Here are some of the right people to ask.

Convention and visitors bureaus (CVBs)

Using CVBs is a great way to save time (and money). CVBs offer lots of great meeting planning services and see your business as a boon to their local economy. Onee of the services they provide, without cost or obligation, is helping you find a suitable (and available) facility, as well as other services providers (such as photographers and local print shops). There are loads of other services they can provide at much lower prices than other vendors. These include housing, collateral publicity materials, transportation, preregistration, and on-site registration. Most CVBs will mail you a very helpful meeting planning guide — full of local information, maps, and event calendars.

To find the CVB in the area, contact the International Association of Convention & Visitors Bureaus (IACVB) at *www.iacvb.org* or (877) Go IACVB ((877) 464-2282). You can request its free directory of destinations and guide with tips on using CVBs. Most CVBs also have Web sites.

National sales offices

Most major hotel chains have national sales offices. These offices can save you lots of time (and money), particularly if you are planning several events in different geographic areas. National sales directors and account managers can quickly check the availability of all of the hotels in their chain to let you know, usually within hours, if there is any space available for your event. You can call directory service at (800) 555-1212 for all the major hotel chains, and you can also find just about all of them online. Many hotels have Web sites that offer assistance with planning, including online floor plans, room capacities, and reservation services. *Successful Meetings* magazine's Web site (*www.successmtgs.com*) has a comprehensive listing of the major hotel chains with links to their Web sites.

Online sources

Log onto *www.meetingsnet.com* for free access to a system called PlanSoft, which has a searchable database of 16,000 meeting facilities throughout North America. You plug in some of the logistics for your meeting and you can find properties that match your needs.

Another site, *www.eventsource.com,* can help you plan conferences, meetings, training, trade shows, and sales and incentive programs. The site's BookIt! e-commerce service is a fast and easy way for users to research and book a meeting with more than 12,000 meeting hotels, convention centers, resorts, and unique venues.

Allmeetings.com is an award-winning national search engine that compares meeting costs (including airfare) at thousands of hotels.

One of the most comprehensive sites on the Web is the Meetings Industry Mall (*www.mim.com*). It can help you find everything meeting related from venues to services to destination information (including currency, weather, and traffic). The site is easy to use and can help you locate available meeting space.

Many times, meeting facilities have open space they can't fill and will offer it at a reduced rate. The Hot Dates Hot

Rates site (*www.hdhr.com*) is the liaison between you and these bargains. This obviously works best if you have a flexible meeting schedule.

Colleagues

It's always worth a try to see if your associates have stayed in particular cities or facilities. Lots of times you're lucky enough to find someone who knows someone who knows someone — you get the idea. It's worth a quick e-mail to your friends and colleagues to let them know what you're looking for.

Types of facilities

Whether it is in a metro area, the suburbs, at the airport, or at a resort, most people just think of hotels. Look beyond hotels. There are many other great venues that could be perfect for your meeting or event. Here's a quick overview of other kinds of meeting space and how to quickly find these more unique meeting facilities.

Conference centers

Conference centers are built to hold meetings, so the meeting space and audiovisual equipment will be state-of-the-art; the sleeping rooms will range from spartan to luxury. A conference center is a great choice for hard-core business meetings with in-depth agendas because all centers are dedicated to helping groups achieve their meeting goals. To see if there's a conference center at the destination you're thinking of, contact the International Association of Conference Centers (*www.iacconline.com*; 314-993-8575).

Convention centers

Convention centers only have function space for meetings, exhibits, and trade shows. They exist solely for large events, usually involving hundreds to thousands of people. However, if you aren't having luck with every other type of meeting facility, it's worth a try.

McCormick Place in Chicago, for example, is the largest convention center in North America. Along with 2.2 million square feet of exhibit halls, it has 114 meeting rooms. Even if there is a huge event taking place, it is likely they might have space for your group. You'll have to look for sleeping rooms elsewhere in the city, of course.

I don't recommend holding smaller meetings in this kind of facility, but sometimes any port in a storm will do. You can find information for convention centers through each state's CVB and, of course, most of them have Web sites.

Colleges and universities

Not only are these sites often more economical than other facilities, but the environments are conducive to learning and you often have access to extras such as campus labs and libraries. Most campus facilities will not confirm space too far in advance, so last minute meeting planners are good candidates for getting space. Housing can vary from dorm rooms to luxury suites. If you don't want use the dorm rooms (and who would?), that's okay; there's usually a decent hotel near campus.

You can find colleges and universities in *The Guide to Unique Meeting Facilities* (*www.theguide.com*; 970-827-5500).

Corporate offices and training centers

Many large companies have training facilities that are available to you for a nominal fee. To date, there is no comprehensive listing available. If you know that you're near a large office building or a corporation's headquarters, though, call and speak with someone either in human resources or in their training department. Two examples of state of the art facilities are The AT&T Learning Center in Basking Ridge, NJ (908-953-3053) and the Xerox Training & Conference Center in Leesburg, VA (703-724-6152). *Training* magazine (*www.trainingsupersite.com*; 612-333-0471) prints a guide listing a lot of these centers.

Corporate offices and training centers have everything you need, except catering, which is easy enough for you to arrange. If there are people coming in from out of town, you can ask the company which hotels they work with and/or recommend.

Other venues

Besides listing conference centers and colleges and universities, *The Guide to Unique Meeting Facilities* (*www.theguide.com*; 970-827-5500) has more than 5,000 unique nontraditional meeting venues throughout North America, including theatres, museums, mansions, retreat centers, and historical and cultural venues.

My last suggestion is bed & breakfasts. These can be a good option, as many have conference facilities in addition to wonderful sleeping rooms. The best compilation, listing approximately 350 inns in North America, is The Innkeepers' Register (*www.innbook.com*; 800-344-5244). CVBs will also have listings of B&Bs.

The booking process

The site inspection

The best way to tell if the sites you're interested in are right for your meeting is to go visit them and do what's known in the meetings industry as "site inspection." On these site inspections you get to meet the hotel person who will be in charge of your meeting. You also get to see if the site is really right for your group (in other words, does the facility match up to the glossy, beautiful pictures in the hotel's brochure or on its Web site?).

As a last minute meeting planner, you're probably not going to have time to do a site inspection, especially if the meeting facility is a plane trip away. A very viable (and recommended) alternative is to have a 15-minute phone conversation with one or two of the facility's key staff. Don't just speak to the sales person; speak to someone in convention services or in the catering department as well. That person will have a different point of view and isn't necessarily interested in selling the facility to you.

Here are some important basic questions that should give you a good comfort level:

- ◷ How old is the property?
- ◷ When was the last renovation? What was done?
- ◷ Will there be any renovation or construction during my meeting? (Jackhammering outside the meeting room will not make your VIPs and executives very impressed with you.)
- ◷ Can you describe the meeting spaces (dimensions and decor)? Can you fax or mail me applicable room diagrams? (You'll want to look for any weird obstructions, such as pillars and

low ceilings. Don't make a final decision until you've seen these diagrams.)

⏱ How long has your staff been with you? (Longevity is a good sign that it is a well-run property.)

⏱ Can you describe the vicinity?

⏱ Are there exclusive suppliers that I have to use (such as for A/V and catering)?

⏱ What other groups are booked in the rooms surrounding mine? (You never know. There may be a cha cha competition next door while your group is deep in a strategy meeting.)

⏱ Are there enough restaurants in the facility to accommodate my group? Are there off-site restaurants within walking distance?

⏱ Are there restrooms and telephones near the meeting room?

⏱ Are there amenities such as pads and pencils provided for each member of my group?

⏱ Can you provide references who had meeting specifications similar to mine?

⏱ What are the cost and availability of transportation and parking?

⏱ Is an up-to-date video or CD-ROM available?

⏱ Will there be any local events happening during my meeting?

⏱ What are the facility's disaster/emergency plans? (The facility will send you its latest reports, if you ask. When I was a new meeting planner, I had an event with 400 people in a resort in Florida. The first night, there was a tornado warning. I called hotel security to ask them what I should do to warn/help my guests. They had no idea what to do in this type of emergency. Neither did the local fire or police departments. Luckily, the tornado never hit. Since then, I never go to an event without emergency procedures in hand.)

Almost every source you encounter will offer a site inspection checklist. An easy one to find, if you want to see what a more a more extensive site selection/inspection checklist looks like can be found at *www.meetingnews.com*, under *Meeting Planner's Handbook*.

The RFP

No matter who's helping you book the space or what kind of facility you've chosen, they're all going to want the same information from you. So, before you start calling anybody or doing any research for space, take a few minutes to fill out a Request for Proposal (RFP). This form outlines for each venue who'll bid on your meeting exactly what you need. You'll include your group's name and contact information; the name and dates of the program/meeting (any flexibility in dates will be to your advantage); the number of attendees you're expecting; background information on the meeting and its history; types of meeting spaces you'll need (including times, room setups, and A/V requirements); and sleeping room requirements. Facilities will then submit proposals to you so that you can select the best fit for your meeting.

The letter of agreement

Once you've booked your space, you'll get a contract or letter of agreement from the hotel. No matter how simple the agreement, do yourself a favor and hire a law firm experienced in reviewing meeting contracts. These firms know, better than anyone, about contractual issues specific to meetings. They will keep an eye out for clauses that you must have in your contract, such as relocation of guests, ADA compliance, attrition, cancellation, renovation or construction, and reciprocal indemnification.

The two big players in the industry are John S. Foster, Esq.(e-mail: jsfoster@mindspring.com; 408-873-5200) and Howe & Hutton (312-263-3001).

While the contract is going through its legal review, you need to look it over as well. Carefully. Are all the dates correct? Does the facility have the right times for your different functions?

Alternative meeting methods

Meeting planning doesn't really go hand-in-hand with "last minute." If you find that there are absolutely no rooms available but you still need to go ahead with your meeting, the Information Age has brought you a couple of options.

Teleconferencing is an easy and inexpensive option if there are just a few (between two and four) people involved, as most office telephone systems can handle that level of teleconferencing. If your meeting involves more people, I suggest using a teleconferencing service. Two I recommend are Conference America (*www.yourcall.com*; 800-925-8000) and AT&T (*www.att.com*; 800-232-1234). Both are good for management meetings, daily calls, financial reviews, customer communications, project and crisis management, and ASAP/ad hoc calls (unanticipated or emergency situations where you must contact everyone).

Audio conferencing just got a whole new look. With this interactive presentation service, audio conferencing is combined with the visual impact of the Internet. Presentations come to life in this live, interactive format. Users actively participate by polling, messaging, viewing the group, requesting the "mic" or responding to the moderator's questions.

Satellite video conferencing is a powerful tool that allows people to communicate face-to-face regardless of geographic separation. In today's highly competitive marketplace, satellite broadcasts are uniting people using either group video systems or personal computers equipped with video capabilities. A good video conferencing resource is AT&T (*www.att.com*; 800-843-3646).

Conclusion

Quick steps

1. Prepare an RFP.
2. Choose a destination.
3. Choose facility types (in order of preference) and send them your RFP.
4. Make a site selection.
5. Review (with your lawyer) the letter of agreement/contract.

Quick tips

☉ Use the Web.
☉ Be as flexible as you can with dates.

Chapter 4

Last Minute Promotions

"Any publicity is good publicity."
— Proverb

No matter what kind of meeting you're planning—be it a planning meeting or a three-day symposium— you need to notify the prospective attendees. When, how, and how often are determined by variables including the meeting type, length, cost, and location, as well as your attendance goals.

Some promotion goals are fixed for you; you're inviting your board of directors to attend the annual board meeting or you're inviting a fellowship to attend their annual banquet. The goals of other events, such as seminars and conferences, are driven by reaching a specific financial or attendance goal. Here your choices of promotion and your invitation list selections require thought and careful selection.

Although successful meeting marketing campaigns can be accomplished by the staff organizing the event, or if you're lucky, a marketing department within your company, you may want to consider hiring an expert. They are well worth the added expenses if your program is especially pricey, unique, or complex. We'll discuss using the services of experts later in this chapter.

The marketing mix

In his *Effective Seminar/Conference Marketing* seminar, Ralph Elliot, Ph.D., advises to "use an integrated marketing mix to maintain an ongoing dialogue with your clients/customers." Are you wondering what the available "mix" is? Tomorrow, ask your department or a few colleagues to collect and pass on to you all the meeting notices they receive during the next week. The variety of the media is fascinating (and full of good ideas you can use). Your choice of materials is only limited by what you can budget for; you'll have to get estimates for copywriting, design, printing, and mailing.

Here's some background on the basic marketing you'll likely see in your in-box next week. Look at it now with an eye towards making your own marketing campaign a success. You'll find copy and design ideas which you'll be able to use in your own promotion efforts.

Direct mail

Direct mail is anything that is written, designed, and either printed and mailed or sent over the Internet. Traditional direct mail notices can be as simple as a photocopied flier on 8 ½ x 11" paper, folded, stapled, stamped, and mailed, or as complex as a four-page sales letter packaged with a 16-page conference brochure and a four-page conference newsletter. Internet direct mail is an e-mail letter with offers and links. Most direct mail pieces for meetings are designed as direct response pieces—meaning that your goal is to get the recipient to respond (by registering or asking for additional information).

The average cost for a direct mail package mailed third class bulk rate—#10 envelope, letter, brochure, order form, and business reply envelope—can reach between $600 and $700 per thousand pieces. This includes printing, list rental, lettershop costs, and postage.

Here's a basic rule of thumb for the timing for a direct mail piece to "hit" your prospects' in-boxes:

- ⏱ Copywriting: two weeks.
- ⏱ Design: two weeks.
- ⏱ Printing: one week.
- ⏱ Shipping from printer to you or your mail house (unless you're using a local printshop): one week.
- ⏱ Transportation from the mail house to get your piece to the post office: one week.
- ⏱ Mailing from the post office to recipients' in-boxes: first-class mail: one week; bulk rate pieces: three to four weeks.

Using this timing, you'd need between seven and 11 weeks. You can, of course, see where you could shave time off the process, allowing you to get information to your prospects more quickly. You could, conceivably, write and design a flier within a day, get it to a local printshop, and have the completed job back in your office by the next day, where you could have your staff slap on address labels and stamps and get it in the mail that day.

Unfortunately, last minute promotions can absolutely hurt attendance because you're not giving people enough notice to plan and budget to attend your event. It's not uncommon for promotion pieces to begin hitting desks as early as six months before an event. Eight to 12 weeks is also common. However, promotions received as late as three or four weeks before an event can work. If your campaign is well-planned, well-written, and well-executed, it can succeed.

Again, watch your own in-box to see samples of direct mail pieces promoting events and inviting you to attend. Common examples include invitations with reply cards, postcards (most useful as "save the date" pieces), newsletters, and brochures. Put yourself on the mailing lists of some of the elite and successful seminar and/or promotion companies and you'll soon compile a file full of strong direct mail pieces you can refer to for ideas.

Some of the mailings I receive include pieces from the Direct Marketing Association, the American Society of Association Executives, and the Professional Convention Management Association. Getting onto your competitors' mailing lists is also a good idea. To learn more about direct marketing, you can contact the Direct Marketing Association, which has offices in New York City (212-768.7277) and Washington, D.C. (202-955.5030). The association's Web site (*www.the-dma.org*) is a rich resource for everything you need to get a direct mail piece done.

Two important considerations are who you're going to mail it to and how you're going to mail it to them.

Mailing lists. The best response will usually come from mailing to your "house list." That simply means the names that you've collected on your database. However, you'll also mail to other prospects who would be good candidates to attend your event. Where do you find these lists? The best way is through a mailing list broker. Brokers specialize in renting mailing lists for direct mail and other marketing promotions.

One of the best known and most reputable list broker services is Edith Roman Associates, Inc. in Pearl River, New York (*www.edithroman.com*). If you want a quick, good education on mailings and mailing lists, visit its informative Web site. To find other mailing list brokers you can try the yellow pages (look under mailing list services) or the Direct Marketing Association's Web site (*www.the-dma.org*).

Mailing. Your organization may have the capability to do mailings in-house. If not, you'll use a mail house (also referred to as a "lettershop"). Lettershops prepare to mail your printed pieces by using equipment that you might not have easy access to, such as inserters, folders, and stamp affixers. Two good sources for finding a mail house are listed under "mailing lists."

Internet direct marketing (e-mail blasts)

E-mail "blasts" — sending a brief e-mail to a list of prospects or clients — can get you the great results that fax campaigns did several years ago. Bob Bly, a freelance copywriter specializing in conventional and Internet direct mail, has seen his pieces get between a 5 and 20 percent click-through, or response rate, with the higher percentages from house lists. Bob has a great article on his Web site (*www.bly.com*) titled *15 Tips for Writing Internet Direct Mail that Works*. His Web site also has a comprehensive list of e-vendors, such as Internet direct mail copywriters, e-list brokers and services bureaus and e-business software companies. You can opt to handle the e-mail blasts yourself — and it's especially easy if you're e-mailing to your own list.

Some magazines have electronic newsletters that accept advertising. If they do, then it is simply a matter of writing a paragraph or two of copy and e-mailing it to them. Make sure you include a link to your event page on your Web site (or at least list your phone number).

Fax blasts

Five or six years ago, fax campaigns were new enough that they got favorably noticed by their recipients, and response rates were high. One association I worked with saved a dying one-day workshop by sending out a last minute fax campaign (five days before the event) and got 20 registrations faxed back, which represented a 12-percent response. Because of successes like these, the medium was much overused and recipients rebelled, saying the campaigns tied up their fax lines and wasted their paper and toner.

If you send well-written faxes (no more than one or two pages), include a response form that can be faxed back to you, and transmit at night when fax machines are idle, direct response faxes are *still* a wonderfully effective and inexpensive last minute push to get people to sign up for your session. (Federal regulations only allow you to send faxes to your customers, the members of your association or group, or people who have requested information about your product or service.)

If you don't have the capabilities to do fax blasts, it is easy and inexpensive to outsource. Smartsource (*www.smartsourceonline.com*; 800-239-0239) is a company I've used with good results. You can also try AT&T's service (*www.webtofax@att.com*) or the American Society of Association Executives (*www.asaenet.org*).

Public Relations (PR)

Why use PR? "Unlike advertising, where there is always a placement cost, PR presents 'free' public exposure of an individual, organization, product, or service via media articles, broadcasts, or public speaker arrangements," explains Jackie Pantaliano, president of ImPRessions Public Relations and Publicity (973-884-4740). PR includes press releases; media tours; speeches and product/service demonstrations; articles; and radio and TV appearances.

For the purposes of promoting an event, the most common form of PR used is the press release (or news release). Pantaliano defines a press release as "typically a one- to three-page announcement of something new, such as an event, seminar, product, service or personnel hire or promotion, whose purpose it is to solicit action (i.e., attend a seminar or event, purchase a product or service, and/or to generate recognition, goodwill, and a positive image)."

A well-written press release will attract the attention of editors, especially those of trade publications who are hungry for material. An article about your event can pay off handsomely. Several years ago, our group was offering a series of seminars at a trade show. We were competing with several other companies who were offering their own seminars simultaneously with ours (which we all agreed to do). Our PR person (who happened to be Jackie Pantaliano) wrote a strong release about our seminars, and it was picked up and printed on the front page of one of the trade show dailies. Our registration that day literally blew the doors off of our competition. And it didn't cost us a cent.

To find PR assistance, you can try one of two New York City–based associations: the Public Relations Society of American (*www.prsa.org*; 212-995-2230) or the Council of Public Relations Firms (*www.prfirms.org*; 877-773-4767)

Another commonly used form of PR for event promotion is the press kit. A press kit is a folder of promotional material distributed to selected media. In meeting and event planning, I've used media kits to invite editors from trade publications to attend our events. Nothing beats a favorable post-event article for building credibility for your organization and your event. The article can be used as a promotional piece for the following year's event or for other promotional purposes.

Advertising

As part of a carefully crafted marketing schedule, advertising can have a powerful impact on your response results. However, it is expensive. A full-page black and white ad in a trade magazine with 72,000 subscribers can cost $3,250. That same ad could cost $24,500 if it's to be run in a consumer magazine with a subscriber base of 500,000.

One option available with your industry trades is a barter. You may be able to barter an ad for free registrations for the publisher or editor-in-chief, for free exhibit space, or for the use of your mailing list.

Telemarketing

According to the book *Guerilla Teleselling* by Jay Conrad Levinson, Orvel Ray Wilson, and Mark S.A. Smith (John Wiley & Sons, 1998), more than 100 million sales calls are made by phone *each week*. These calls generate $370 billion in sales annually.

A percentage of these sales belongs to the revenue generated by meetings. In the case of telemarketing your seminar, the calls made won't be "cold calls" but rather calls to discuss the upcoming event and to generate interest in attending.

There may be people on your staff who can do this, but telemarketing skills take time to develop, and the process needs to be carefully scripted out. Consult trade magazines, the Direct Marketing Association, and watchdog agencies such as American Telemarketing Association and Telewatch to find reputable firms.

Marketing tasks

As I mentioned in Chapter 1, I keep two detailed lists: an action plan outlining every to-do item and a marketing plan to keep me on schedule and make sure that every promotion is created and mailed on time. Figure 4.1 is an example of part of an actual promotion schedule used for a five-day annual conference with a goal of drawing 300 people. The complete schedule would include other promotional venues (such as telemarketing, Web promotions, and fax and e-mail blasts) as well as your advertising and press release plans.

Figure 4.1

Widget Top Management Conference Promotion Schedule (as of 8/23)

I. DIRECT-MAIL PLAN:

PROMOTION PIECE	DESIGN BY DATE	PRINTED BY DATE	MARKET SEGMENT	MAIL CLASS	DROP DATE	HIT DATE
POSTCARD #1	7/7	7/98	- WIDGET members: 3,100 -Past attendees (non-members) -GLS members (CPIA, PICA, PIAMS, NAGASA, PIVA, and GAA)	bulk	7/98	8/98
WTMC 99 Newsletter Vol. 1, No. 1	8/26	9/9	-Past WTMC attendees (96, 97, 98): 400 -Inquiries: 300 -WIDGET Members: 3500 -TPX rented list: 8,000 -GLS members/prospects (CPIA, PICA, PIAMS, NAGASA, PIVA, and GAA): 4,100 (450 members/1,100 CPIA)	first/bulk	9/18	10/7

BROCHURE mails with letter	9/8	10/9	-Past WTMC attendees (96, 97, 98) -Inquiries -WIDGET Members -TPX rented list selection: 8,000 -Graph Expo listing of top executives in West Cost -GLS members/prospects	first/ bulk	10/19	10/28
WTMC 99 Newsletter Vol.1, No. 2	9/7	9/18	-Past WTMC attendees (96, 97, 98) -Inquiries -WIDGET Members -TPX rented list selection: 8,000 -GLS members/prospects	bulk	9/30	10/15
BROCHURE **NOTE: same content, different cover**			- Past WTMC attendees (96, 97, 98) -Inquiries -WIDGET Members *(RIDE IN 11/15 MEMBER MAILING)* -TPX rented list selection: 8,000 -GLS members/prospects	bulk	10/30	11/15
POSTCARD #2 (promote keynote)	7/7	7/98	-12/15 Widget member mailing: 3,100 -Past attendees (nonmembers) -GLS members	bulk	11/15	11/30
Brochure	n/a	n/a	-Peer Groups with letter from Robin -other special groups?	first	11/98	11/98
POSTCARD #3 (promote end of early bird rates)	7/7	7/98	-WIDGET members:3,100 -Past attendees (non-members) -GLS members	bulk	12/1	12/15

Promotional writing

Promotional pieces, including PR, are often written in-house. This is fine, if you have experienced copywriters and PR people on staff. Otherwise, consider outsourcing. If you're tight on time and you're inexperienced, you won't be making good use of your time by writing in-house — and you won't get the same results as a professional will. Search the industry supplier section on the DMA's Web site. You can also contact the Copywriter's Council in Middle Island, NY (631-924-8555) for referrals.

Design

You may want to try your hand at designing your own material, but unless you're a skilled designer, please don't! As New Jersey–based graphic design professional Cathy Vitale (201-569-9559) noted, "With today's computer tech craze, everybody is under the impression that if they just buy a design program at an office supply store, they can have their secretary design their material. And we all know what that ends up looking like!" Vitale added, "You have to get people to want to be at *your* event and not somebody else's. You do that by creating a mood, an atmosphere. You need to let your prospect know what kind of company is putting on this event. To do that, you have to make the piece look good." The bottom line is there are many other events out there touting the same type of content. People to come to yours because yours looks professional and credible — and designers make that happen.

To find designers, ask for referrals and check the yellow pages, trade magazines, or the American Institute of Graphic Artists (*www.aiga.org*; 212-807-1990). Copywriter Bob Bly also has a list on his Web site (*www.bly.com*) under "vendors."

Tip: When the designer gives you a comp, or dummy, of your piece, take it to your local post office and speak to the people in charge of mailings. They will look at your piece and make sure it meets postal regulations. (Have the person sign off on the piece.) If you don't, the postal service may not be able to deliver your mail.

Printing

Your options include printing it yourself (not advised unless you have a good quality laser or digital printer), having it printed by a local quick printshop, or using a regular printing company. Unless there's a reason not to (for example, you need a type of specialty printing that they don't handle, such as 3-D), choose from your company's current vendors. If you do need to find a new printer you can check your local phone book or call one of the printing industry's trade associations. They can't give referrals, but they can give you a list of their members in your area.

Tip: If you're printing something to be distributed during your event (like an awards banquet program) consider having it printed in that city. Paper is heavy, so you'll save money on shipping charges.

Conclusion

Quick steps

1. Decide on your marketing mix.
2. Create a marketing schedule.
3. Hire vendors and give them their piece of the project in a timely way so that you stay on track. The same courtesy should be extended to in-house staff.

Quick tips

- Use experts as much as possible—but know they can be expensive.
- Your mailing list is the most critical element to the success rate of your promotional efforts.
- The best list is almost always your "house list."

Chapter 5

Finding and Hiring Speakers

"Experience is one thing you can't get for nothing."
—Oscar Wilde

Your meeting program plan will help you determine if you need speakers, and if so, how many and what type (for example, motivational, specialist, or outside expert). These choices can make or break the success of the event. Now your search begins. Luckily, there are lots of places to turn to find a speaker—even at the last minute.

Where the speakers are

Speaker bureaus

Speaker bureaus represent speakers and handle the logistics for the speakers (including their contract, their travel, and their audiovisual needs). They can make your life easier because they're the experts in selecting appropriate speakers for groups. A few caveats: Take the time to review video tapes and ask bureaus for speaker references (and call them!); make sure you'll have the opportunity to speak with the speaker both before you make the hire and then again sometime after the hire; and have your lawyer review the speaker's contract.

Here are four of the top agencies. I've used two of them (the Leigh Bureau and Greater Talent Network) with good results; the other two both have a good reputation. The Leigh Bureau in Bridgewater, N.J. (*www.leighbureau.com*; 908-253-6033) has been around for more than 70 years and is a first-class organization. Greater Talent Network in New York City (*www.greatertalent.com*; 800-326-4211) has been in the business of representing speakers for nearly 20 years. If you have the time, you can ask for either bureau's free speaker catalog. Both are beautifully written, designed, and printed pieces with lots of fascinating information about people on the speaking circuit.

Another well-known bureau is the International Speakers Bureau in Dallas (*www.isbspeakers.com*; 800-842-4483), which represents 15,000 speakers. Lastly is Leading Authorities, Inc., headquartered in Washington, D.C. (*www.leadingauthorities.com*; 800-SPEAKER), with 800 names in its database.

Even thought it isn't a speaker bureau, the National Speakers Association (*www.nsaspeaker.org*), located in Tempe, Ariz., can be a gold mine for you. It has 37 local chapters, too. You contact the association to search for one of its 3,800 speakers—by location, topic, name, budget constraints, and so forth. Once you've found some matches, you'll contact and work with the speaker directly.

Authors

Recently, an association I was working with was looking for a keynote speaker. The program chair happened upon an article in *GQ* magazine about a new book whose topic would make for an interesting, controversial keynote. (The book was *Taboo: Why Black Athletes Dominate Sports and Why We Are Afraid to Talk About It* by Jon Entine.) We contacted Jon directly. Although we did finally book him with the speaker bureau he worked with, many authors are independents. Keep your eyes open for new, interesting books, articles, and essays. Authors are generally eager to speak to groups.

Associations

Literally *any* topic you can think of will be covered by an association. Listings of associations can be found through the American Society of Association Executives (*www.asaenet.org*; 202-626-ASAE). You can also check your local library's copy of Gale's Encyclopedia of Associations and National Organizations of the U.S. Your contact at an association will probably be the education or meetings director, who will be able to direct you to speakers within the industry. The speakers will range from board members to consultants to industry leaders and/or experts. Additionally, many associations and groups have their own speakers bureaus.

Marketing/Public relations departments

Looking for a big Kahuna to speak at your event—Bill Gates, perhaps? The easiest place to start is with his company's marketing or public relations department. These departments are used to handling such requests and can give you the guidelines you need to hire one of its company's executives.

Other sources: CVBs, colleagues, board members, experts in your industry

The Convention & Visitors Bureau from the city/state you're holding your meeting will be able to provide you with a list of local speakers. A big plus to finding a speaker in the geographic region is the savings on airfare and other travel-related costs. One association I worked with hired a keynote speaker from Seattle to present an hour and a half session in Maryland. The airfare alone was more than $2,000.

If you're going to ask board or committee members or colleagues for ideas and referrals, you should put together a one-page brief about the program and the kind(s) of speakers you're searching for. It you're looking for a keynote, it would be helpful to also give a listing of previous speakers.

The Basics of Hiring a Speaker

Here are eight tips to ensure you're hiring the right speaker to fit your program's content, budget, and format:

1. Ask the speaker for his background material. Review his client list and outlines of talks to get a feel for his style.
2. Remember: WYSIWYG (what you see is what you get). Get one or two videotapes of presentations. An audio cassette is okay in a pinch. Even better, if time permits, is to go see the speaker in action.
3. Call the speaker's references. Speak to at least three. Try to speak to people who held meetings similar to yours; what worked at an

incentive meeting in Maui might not at an educational symposium in Chicago.

4. Speak to the speaker personally. Once you hire the speaker, you'll be communicating at least four or five times before your event. Rapport is important. So is knowing if the speaker knows his stuff and has the right kind of personality for your group. Find out if and how he will tailor his information for your group. Finally, make sure the speaker is able to speak for the length of time you envision. A novice planner I know recently booked a speaker for a three-hour keynote session. It wasn't until she received the contract that she found out he could only speak on the topic for 90 minutes! (They resolved the matter by having him present two different topics in the three-hour time frame.)

5. Find out what kind of travel costs will be associated with the presentation *before you hire the speaker*. These can be some of the "hidden costs" that blow your budget. Some speakers insist on first class bookings; some will refuse to take an extra travel day to save money on transportation.

6. Find out about A/V needs, another "hidden cost" to get out in the open. Some speakers only want a lavaliere microphone (regular small clip-on microphone) and an overhead projector (costing only a couple hundred dollars); others will require elaborate setups involving rear screen projections and special sound and lighting (costing upwards of $2–3,000). This is important to discuss up front.

7. Discuss fees. Industry speaker fees can range from gratis gigs to $500 or $750 for a one- or

two-hour session to $1,000 or more. Well-known industry speakers command more; some charge upwards of $3,000 to $5,000. Non-celebrity authors might charge in the $5,000 to $7,000 range. Fees for keynote speakers will typically range from $7,500 to $100,000. Do these rates seem high? Remember that you're not only paying for this person's expertise; you're also paying for his time. If a consultant could be on a consulting assignment but chooses to speak at your event instead, he needs to be paid accordingly.

8. Have a contingency plan in place in the event of a no-show speaker. Although it happens rarely, sometimes speakers don't show up. Require your speakers to arrive the night before their sessions. That way, if they don't show up, you have some time to work on a resolution. In the case of keynote speakers, always have a clause in your contract stating that the speaker bureau must supply a replacement speaker of equal caliber. For a no-show, call your contact at the speaker bureau to have them get you a replacement. (Make sure you have the contact's after hours/emergency phone and pager numbers.) No-shows are a rarity, because speakers' careers depend on their reliability. But make contingency plans *before you're on site* just in case.

Get Your money's worth

If you're hiring a keynote, you're usually paying for either a half-day or full day of his time. Some tips to getting your money's worth include asking the keynote to present at a special breakfast for a select group, facilitate a panel discussion at another time slot, or hold a book signing. Or if he is coming for the keynote, have him also do a breakout. If he is coming for a half-day morning seminar, ask him to speak at lunch.

Communicating with your speakers

You'll be communicating with your speakers via phone, fax, and e-mail while planning your program. Once you've hired a speaker, you'll send a follow-up confirmation (also known as a contract or a letter of agreement). The purpose is to put important details in writing to make sure you both heard, understood, and agree to the items discussed during your phone call.

The contract

The contract is a legal document and requires signatures. Figure 5.1 is a contract in the form of a letter of agreement.

Figure 5.1

Dear [NAME]:

We are looking forward to our Top Management Conference and your participation as a presenter. You were chosen to speak at this showcase event because of your industry knowledge, your experience, and your outstanding presentation skills. We're happy to have your support of this conference. Listed below are facts relating to your speaking engagement and the 1999 Top Management Conference.

Logistical Information:

Dates: The Top Management Conference is Wednesday, February 17–Sunday, February 21. The full conference brochure is enclosed. This year's theme is "the future direction of the widget industry." Our focus is to help widget manufacturers manage the new technologies, fuel up for growth and opportunity, and maintain the spirit of their organizations. Expected attendance is 200 Widget executives and their guests.

Location: Four Seasons Biltmore
1260 Channel Drive
Santa Barbara, CA 93108
Phone: 805/969-2261
Fax: 805/969-4682

Travel: We've reserved a sleeping room for you at the Four Seasons Biltmore

Arrival: [DAY/DATE]

Departure: [DAY/DATE]

Please let us know if this is incorrect.

Please arrange your own travel; see compensation information below.

Your Presentation:

You are scheduled to present the following: [NAME OF SESSION(S)]

Dates/Times:

Fees: You will receive a speaking fee of $xxx and will be reimbursed for travel expenses (including hotel) for up to $xxx. You are entitled to compensation up to, but not exceeding, $xxx. You also receive a complimentary conference registration, valued at $xxx.

Handouts: If you would like the Widget Company to copy and ship your handouts, please send a clean copy of the handouts to us by Wednesday, January 27, 1999.

Audiovisual: See attached form.

Your breakout session is 1 1/2 hours in length and we have a limited audiovisual budget. If you feel your session requires "high-tech" A/V such as LCD panels or computers, please call me at [PHONE NUMBER] to discuss.

This agreement is subject to the terms and conditions stated below:

* Confirmation Agreement Letter to be returned to WIDGET COMPANY within 15 days of the date hereof.

* Any audiovisual equipment needed for the program that is not listed on the attached Audio-Visual Equipment Request Form submitted to WIDGET COMPANY will not be paid for by WIDGET COMPANY.

* If special audiovisual equipment is ordered by the speaker and not used, WIDGET COMPANY reserves the right to charge the speaker for the equipment rental.

* Speakers are not authorized to order their own audiovisual equipment from the facility where the meeting is being held. If this occurs, the speaker will be responsible for the payment of this equipment.

* The above compensation is for a one-time agreement between WIDGET COMPANY and the Speaker, and unless agreed to in writing, does not include miscellaneous charges for an assistant, spouse, or friend.

* WIDGET COMPANY will not pay for valet or laundry charges, Pro Shop or Gift Shop charges.

* WIDGET COMPANY will not pay for materials that have been reproduced by the speaker unless approved in advance.

* Payment will be issued 30-60 days following receipt of a statement for professional services.

* Speakers are asked to refrain from marketing their products or services.

* Please plan your schedule so that you can meet and greet attendees prior to your presentation and stay afterwards to answer questions.

* In the event that the program is canceled, WIDGET COMPANY will not be responsible for fees or expenses

incurred for this seminar by the speaker. Cancellations will be made prior to the program date.

* WIDGET COMPANY must receive your complete invoice within 15 days following the speaking engagement
* **WIDGET COMPANY will not pay invoices that do not have receipts attached for any charges exceeding $20.00.**
* WIDGET COMPANY has my permission to audiotape my presentation and make it available to attendees.

        Yes   No   Initial

We look forward to working with you at the Top Management Conference. Thank you for your continued commitment and support of WIDGET COMPANY.

Warm Wishes,

_____

Fern Dickey, CMP, Director, Widget Education
ACCEPTED BY:

_____   _____

Speaker   Date of Acceptance

    Some contracts will be more detailed, but many will be less. Some additional clauses to consider adding include:

- ⏱ **Sales.** You'll stipulate whether or not your company will allow speakers to sell their products, distribute literature about their company, or make mention of their products or services during their presentation. Note: If you are going to let them sell their products, you might want to buy their products yourself (at a discount) and sell or give them to the attendees. Sometimes speakers will even agree to just give you a cut of their revenue earned if they sell the products themselves.

🕐 **Dress Code.** Every speaker I've worked with has dressed appropriately for the occasion. They are professionals and will be looking to make a good impression. However, always send them the conference or event brochure so they can read what the accepted attire will be. You can put something in the contract if you feel it is necessary.

As with any legal document, check with your legal counsel before you use it. A tip for the contract and all other forms and material you will need from the speaker: Pad your deadline by at least two weeks. Speakers are busy and on the road quite a bit, and you'll need time to call them to remind them to return material to you.

Because of my experience with some speakers who never get back to me, I usually put three caveats on my material to speakers:

1. If I don't get their handouts by the due date (which I will renegotiate into a "drop-dead" due date when I speak with them, which I follow · up on in writing), they are responsible for copying and getting their handouts to the program — at their own expense.

2. If they don't give me their audiovisual requests before the program, their room will be set with basic equipment (that is, a lavaliere microphone, a lectern, an overhead project, a screen, and a flipchart.) They cannot order additional equipment on site unless they pay for it.

3. Unless otherwise specified, they are to purchase advance, coach-class round-trip tickets. Usually, I just put a cap, based on reasonable (and researched) current rates, on travel expenses, which I've found to be the easiest way to handle this.

Speaker Information Forms

Send a Speaker Information Form with your contract. This document is filled out by the speaker and sent back to you along with the contract. It covers all kinds of specifics: contact information, audiovisual requirements, meeting room setup needs, taping refusal/authorization, travel arrangement information (airline and hotel), and biographical information.

Handout material copyrights

In addition to sending the speaker your agreement, speaker information form and material about your company and/or event, it is important to include a handout copyright release form. You can get one from Kinko's or Sir Speedy. The speaker fills out and signs the form, which gives you permission to copy and distribute his material. Some copy centers—particularly those near colleges and universities—are sticklers for asking for these forms before they copy your material.

Other mailings

Once you receive your printed promotional material, send it to your speakers. Using a cover letter gives you an opportunity to reiterate dates and other important information (such as reminders to make travel arrangements) which will help you help speakers stay on track.

Your final written correspondence will be your thank-you letter, preferably sent with the speaker's evaluation. A brief letter is all that's necessary, but this important final task shouldn't be neglected.

Scheduled calls

In addition to the calls made during the initial hiring process, you should have periodic conversations with your speakers.

Particularly with keynote speakers, plan a conference call between the speaker and other important members of your organization, including your executive staff or executive committee. Prepare a brief agenda. The purpose of this call is to help the speaker tailor his presentation. You'll accomplish this by acquainting the speaker with your industry, industry hot topics, and an understanding of the knowledge level of the audience.

You should give the speaker a final call a few (three or four) weeks prior to the event to confirm the date and time of his session and to review travel arrangements and other details. Give the speaker a comfort level by letting him know where he can pick up his registration material, who will meet him in his meeting room to review the room setup, and who will be introducing him.

You'll be making a lot of miscellaneous calls to the speaker to track down contracts, speaker information forms, handout material, and to go over changes in programs or news you want to impart. It's time-consuming, but keeping your speakers in the loop ensures success during your event.

Successful presentations

Although it's best to let experts do their thing, there are some things you can do to help your speakers succeed — particularly for those speakers who have been selected because they are subject matter experts and not professional speakers.

Pre-meeting

Ask to review an advance copy of the speaker's presentation or outline. There are two reasons for doing so: to make sure you have it in time to produce copies for the meeting (in the event that you'll be distributing handouts) and to make sure the material doesn't contain anything too saleslike, off-color, or inappropriate for your group or organization. Once, I had a speaker use handouts that made mention (many, many times) of a competing trade association and never mentioned ours!

If the speaker is planning a panel session, suggest phone rehearsals. It is particularly helpful to have a conference call so that the panelists can talk over the issues to be discussed, decide who's going to cover particular points, and so forth. It will make the actual session more fluid and educational.

Help speakers understand the size of the room they'll be in. If you don't, they may prepare material that only the first few rows can see.

Give the speakers some generic tips about projecting material to the audience. These guidelines from the Professional Meeting Management (third edition, published by the Professional Convention Management Association) are brief yet helpful:

- ☺ The accepted standard in A/V artwork with a 6" x 9" information area is that no character should be less than 1/8" in height.
- ☺ The 6 x 6 rule maximizes readability: no more than six words per line and six lines per page of text.
- ☺ The use of upper and lower case letters in the body copy is much easier to read than all upper case text.

☉ Flip charts only work with small groups. For larger groups, use an overhead projector.

If the speaker is going to offer a Q&A period, ask him to prepare some sample questions for you to "plant" in the audience. This is very helpful in getting the ball rolling (and it saves the speaker the embarrassment of dead air!). If you have a large room, make sure you have microphones for the audience so their questions can be heard throughout the room.

Make sure speakers know the break times and end times of their sessions. It is important to keep a program on schedule and it is unfair to the speaker who'll be using the room next.

On site

Greet the keynote speaker. It's a nice gesture on behalf of your organization, plus, you've communicated so many times you're probably old friends by now. You or other executive staff may make arrangements to share a meal with the speaker. You can give the speaker a venue orientation, give him his badge and on-site materials, and review any last minute issues. If there is going to be an extensive audiovisual setup for the speaker, the venue will set it up the night before. Often, you'll arrange to meet the speaker again in the late evening to look over the room.

It's usually not possible to meet each speaker as they arrive. I call their rooms to make sure they're checked in and to make sure they're comfortable and ready to go. (For the most part, I require my speakers to arrive the night before. That way, I have an early heads-up if they're not going to make the meeting and I can begin making other arrangements to fill their time slot.)

Provide a speaker ready room. This room is filled with audiovisual equipment. It's purpose is to give the speakers a place to rehearse, review, and double-check their presentation materials. I've only used speaker ready rooms at trade shows, when we were running upwards of 100-plus sessions. Otherwise, I don't—usually because there isn't enough money in the budget to do so. However, if you can, it is a big plus for the speakers.

Allow for adequate setup time. Particularly if you don't have a speaker ready room, make sure there is enough time between sessions for speakers to get into their rooms, set up, and test the equipment. Most breaks run from 15 to 30 minutes. You can decide based on the complexity of the audiovisual equipment you're using.

Include speaker introductions. Even for small breakout sessions, it is a courteous and professional touch. According to Stephen D. Boyd, a professor of speech education at Northern Kentucky University, "The primary purpose of our introduction is to qualify the speaker as an expert on the topic to be discussed." Introductions should be brief, less than a minute, except for keynote introductions, which can be as long as two or three minutes. (See Chapter 11 for more information.) Boyd suggests having these three elements in your introduction: the subject being addressed; the significance of the topic; and information about the speaker. End your introduction with a chance for the audience to applaud—something like, "Let's give Mr. X a warm welcome." Ask speakers to forward their own introductions for you to read. This way, you don't have to take the time to prepare them; you only have to edit the different speakers' introductions for consistency.

Conclusion

Quick steps

1. Select speakers based on your program and budget.
2. Send each speaker a contract, a copyright release form, and information about your event and your organization.
3. Communicate regularly via phone calls, letters, or e-mail.

Quick tips

☉ Don't hire a speaker without seeing a tape or a live session.

☉ Make sure you're prepared if a speaker doesn't show up.

☉ Keep audiovisual requests in check.

Chapter 6

Working with the Facility

Your meeting is booked through a member of the venue's sales department. Once your contract is signed, your event will be turned over to either the catering director or, more typically, a convention and services manager (CSM).

The CSM will work with you during your pre-event planning process, on site during your event, and then afterward as you prepare post-conference reports and review the final invoice from the facility. Establishing a good working relationship is key. This person will be a close colleague and your guardian angel—helping you through problems that will inevitably occur before and during your meeting.

The players

The CSM

Every facility's CSM has a slightly different title and handles slightly different responsibilities. However, for the most part, this is the person who will be your liaison with other departments (banquets, front desk, catering, and so on) until you are on site. Additionally, many CSMs are experienced meeting planners, and oftentimes have earned the CMP designation (Certified Meeting Professional). They can advise and guide you as you plan your event.

Let the CMS know that you're planning a last minute event. He'll tell you what he handles and when you should work directly with another department. The CSM will work with you to establish deadlines to make sure your meeting gets planned on schedule.

Keep in touch with the CSM. Send him your event's promotional materials. It helps him understand your group and your event. In return, he'll send you a comprehensive packet about the venue. This should include maps with layouts and capacities of the meeting rooms, menus, the audiovisual rental list, a list of services that the venue offers (a morning paper and complimentary airport shuttle, for example), and on-site restaurant outlets.

Catering department

Believe it or not, catering and banquet departments *are* different departments. Catering handles the food and beverage. Sometimes you'll talk in advance to the catering director if you need to plan a special function, would like to serve something that's not on the menu, or are working with a very tight budget and need ideas for creative, low-cost meals.

Banquet department

These are the folks who set up and break down your function rooms — the chairs, tables, and stages. You'll work with them constantly on site, because you'll be calling on them to make changes to rooms, add more chairs, bring garbage cans to work rooms, remove boxes during set up, move tables into different configurations, and so on. A banquet captain is the person in charge of banquet service at your food function, setting up tables and chairs, making sure the proper linens are being used, and so on. It's important to find out if there is a union, because unions have strict regulations — you cannot move even a desk without a union employee being present.

Audiovisual (A/V) department

You will definitely speak with this department before your event. You'll want to make sure you're aware of, and understand, every fee — especially "hidden" fees for things such as outlets and extension cords. For example, at the last conference I planned, the hotel tried to charge us $10 a day for every outlet we used in an exhibit room. We were able to settle without paying the extra fee. Try to negotiate to have the little items (such as outlets and cords) be complimentary. You'll also talk with the A/V department about special setups. If, for example, your keynote speaker has special lighting and intensive projection equipment or if you'll need technicians to stay in a meeting room during an important presentation as a precautionary measure, you want to let the A/V department know as soon as possible so that they can make arrangements before the event.

Reservations department

Even if you've outsourced the housing reservation process, you'll still be talking to the reservations staff as you plan your event. They'll be sending you room reports letting you know how your "pick up" (how many rooms have sold per night against how many rooms you guaranteed) is. In return, you'll be faxing them your rooming list, which may just be your staff and VIPs if you've outsourced the rest.

As your contracted cutoff date closes in, you'll work together to closely monitor the rooms available to your group. If the hotel is beginning to look like it is almost sold out and your room block is almost closed, too, you may opt to reserve a few extra rooms just in case the hotel becomes sold out. On the other hand, if registration for your meeting isn't going well (and therefore people aren't reserving rooms), you'll be in constant touch to see how the hotel is faring in selling your rooms once they're back in the general inventory.

Figure 6.1 shows a sample rooming list (although most lists would have more names than this!).

Figure 6.1

Widget Conference
National Association of Widget Engineers
Hotel Room Roster as of June 6
for the Crystal Gateway Marriott

REGISTRATION DATE	NAME	ROOM TYPE	ARR. DATE	DEP. DATE	# OF NIGHTS
May 15	Joe Speaker	SINGLE	6/29	6/31	2
	Company				
	Address	NOTES: Nonsmoking room.			
	City, State, Zip	Place one (1) hotel room night & tax to			
	Fax	Master Account.			
		Phone and Incidentals to individual.			
		Credit Card # xxx xxxx xxx xxxx			
May 15	Fern Dickey	SINGLE	6/24	6/31	7
	NAWE				
	Address	NOTES: Complimentary room per contract.			
	City, State, Zip	All charges to the Master Account.			
	Phone	Nonsmoking room.			
	Fax				

2 records for the hotel   TOTAL ROOM NIGHTS: 9

Others departments

You can talk with your CSM about the other departments in the hotel and the roles that each play. Here's a brief list.

Front Desk. This department handles sleeping room registrations and serves as a cashier. You or your CSM should talk to the front desk manager about your peak arrival date to double check that the front desk is properly staffed. It's also a good idea to give the front desk a list of your VIPs.

Bell Staff. They primarily carry luggage but are also available to help you with other tasks, such as running errands, delivering boxes to you from shipping if shipping is unavailable, or dropping off materials to guest rooms.

Concierge. This person (or staff of people) provides services to guests, such as help with restaurant reservations, procuring tickets to local events, and making transportation arrangements.

Security. This department maintains safety on the property.

Engineering. This is the building's maintenance staff. Something that's good to know is that they control the room temperatures. (You'll usually *only* talk to them when your rooms are too hot or too cold!)

Housekeeping. This department maintains guest rooms.

Shipping Department. Here's where all your boxes will be delivered and stored until you're on site. This department will also take care of shipping your boxes back to your office after the event. (You'll pack and label them, fill out a form, and then let the shipping department take over.)

Business Center. If you need assistance at the last minute, this department is a blessing — but you'll pay dearly for its services.

Switchboard. These are the in-house operators.

Accounting. You'll probably talk to this department once or twice when you're setting up your Master Account, and you probably won't talk to Accounting again until you're reviewing your final invoice from the facility.

MOD. This isn't a department, but a person. The Manager on Duty (MOD) is the person in charge of the hotel after business hours. Make sure you know who this will be each evening and the best way to reach him.

Things to know

In this section we'll concentrate on the different services you'll be using through the venue.

Audiovisual

I've always been lucky and have had great facilities' staffs that I trusted to order the appropriate equipment for the size of the crowd. Here are some basic audiovisual rules you can follow to make sure everyone in the room will be able to hear the speaker, see the screen, and feel like part of the action. You're not really going to measure, but you'll be able to look at the setup and see if something looks very wrong.

☺ The average person is 4′ 6″ in a seated position, so the screen must start at five feet off the ground for everyone to see the entire screen.

☺ The 2x8 guideline: The first row of attendees should not be any closer than (a) two times the screen height (a six-foot screen, therefore, means 12 feet of empty space before the first row) and (b) the last row must be within eight times the screen height in order to see the screen (so a six-foot screen can accommodate rows within 48 feet of the screen.)

Two tips:

1. Make sure you've asked for complimentary setup in your contract. Hotels will sometimes charge you to set up chairs, tables, and A/V equipment if you don't request otherwise.

2. If you don't see package prices listed on the equipment rental info, ask for them. If you're ordering an overhead projector, you'll also need a cart (to place it on) and a screen. It costs more to order them à la carte than it does to order them as an equipment package.

Food and beverage

There have been volumes written regarding food and beverage. This is because meals are a major expense and there are so many types of meals and variables. You aren't going to have time to read and digest all this material (pardon the pun), so here's the speedy way to plan your meal functions.

Begin by sending your program format (see Figure 1.1) to your CSM and ask him to review it. He can tell you if you've allotted enough time for food functions, breaks, and special events (such as banquets). Here are some timing rules of thumb:

Breaks. Allot a minimum of a half hour after every one and a half hours of session time. You might just want people to grab a cup of coffee and come back into the room, but your attendees need to stretch their legs, call the office, and use the rest rooms. A 15-minute break is acceptable if there are a series of two or three short breakout sessions that people are attending.

Breakfast. A continental breakfast needs between a half hour and one hour. A breakfast buffet needs at least an hour; one and a half hours is better. A full served breakfast can last between one and one and a half hours.

Lunch. You'll need one and a half hours, unless it is an awards or special luncheon, in which case you'll need to allow two hours.

Receptions. Allow 45 minutes to one hour. One and a half hours is okay; two hours is too long (and too expensive if you're paying the tab).

Dinner. Allow two hours for a regular sit-down meal. You'll need three hours for a themed event (with dancing or entertainment). An awards dinner needs about four hours.

Next, go through the venue's menus and begin picking and choosing your type of meal and type of service. For each event, you'll need to give the hotel the time, number of expected guests, how you'd like the room set up, and your choice of food and beverage.

Figure 6.2 is a sample, with comments in italics, of how you'll plug the information into a format that you'll present to the hotel in a meeting specifications document. (Read more about meeting specs later in this chapter.) The "++" you'll see means "plus tax and plus gratuity" and is standard.

Figure 6.2

Date: Monday, May 5

Time: 12:00 noon–4:00 p.m.

Event: Board of Directors Luncheon Meeting

The time and event had already been decided during the planning stage.

Location: El Jardin/La Loma

You may request a specific room or you can let the venue choose for you.

Covers: 32

This is the number you are guaranteeing (and paying for). If you have a history of the meeting, this number is easier to determine. Numbers may fluctuate year to year due to weather, nearby attractions, or a number of other reasons. Most venues need you to give them your final *number between 48 and 72 hours before the event. You can almost always increase the number after that. You can never decrease the guarantee. Hotels will usually set up between 3 and 5 percent more seats than your number, which gives you some flexibility.*

Setup: Hollow Square

        1 easel outside room

See diagram.

This session needs to be taped.

These are your instructions to the hotel. The Hollow Square refers to how I wanted the room set up. See more below about your options.

F&B: Lunch Buffet: Working Lunch Two**

Albacore tuna and bow tie pasta salad, Caesar salad with Foccacia croutons; assorted specialty bread sandwiches: turkey club with avocado, grilled Mediterranean vegetable, Italian cold cut with provolone; dill pickles, olives and pepperoncinis; basket of vegetable chips; brownies, cookies and apple squares; whole fresh fruit

(**This is $28.00++ pp. **Please give me price without beef and barley soup and red cabbage slaw.**) Does the 50-person minimum apply? If so, please suggest alternate lunch option.

Iced tea at $10.00++ per pitcher, sodas and mineral waters at $3.00++ & $3.25++ on consumption.

I actually copy my entire menu choice onto my own specifications. A lot of meeting planners don't. It may seem time-consuming, but it actually makes the checking and final rechecking of the venue's job order (officially called the Banquet Event Order or BEO) much faster and easier. Note that I had to work within a budget, so I asked for some help to lower the cost of the meal. You can, and should, play around with menus to suit your attendees and your budget. It is always cheaper, but not always possible, to buy by the gallon or pitcher or tray vs. buying per person.

People are either served by waiters or stand on a buffet line. If you offer a buffet, talk with the facility to make sure it is set up properly so that there isn't going to be a long line. They'll suggest stations around the room or a single buffet with adequate room for people to form lines on either side of the table.

Besides the food functions you plan, there may be some meals where attendees are "on their own." You must find out — particularly if it's a lunch in the middle of a work-shop — if the venue's on-site food facilities can handle the number of people in your group. You'll be the center of attention if attendees haven't been able to eat lunch because the wait at the restaurant was too long.

Room setups

There are many ways to set up your meeting room. Think about the kind of session you're planning. Is there going to be a lecture where people will be taking notes, a small board meeting, a small discussion, or work groups? There are four basic setups, each with possible variations.

1. Theatre (or auditorium). Similar to a movie theatre, the setup consists of rows of chairs placed next to one another. There are no tables. This kind of seating is typical for large keynote sessions or lectures. It's not for any kind of "hands-on" learning.

2. Classroom (or schoolroom). This setup consists of rows of tables and chairs and is typically used for educational sessions, whether large or small.

    For both theatre and classroom setups, a typical (and nice) variation is for the side rows to be angled in (usually called either chevron or herringbone) to face the stage.

3. Rounds (or banquet). This setup consists of chairs around round tables.

    A common variation is for the tables have four or five chairs set on just one side of the table (and facing the stage). It works well for a fairly large room in two ways. It lets the audience work in small groups, and it makes it easy for the venue to "turn the room over" and get it ready for a meal function.

4. Conference (or boardroom). This setup consists of chairs set around a large table (usually oval) or chairs and tables set into a hollow square, allowing up to 25 or 30 people to meet for an interactive discussion.

Rules of thumb:

1. Each person needs about two feet of space. If people are going to be writing in notebooks, three feet is better. This figures to two or three people per six-foot table (and three or four people per eight-foot table). Six-foot tables are more commonly used, and seating just two people at each table is comfortable.

2. When you're setting any kind of square conference style, make sure you only have one person per corner.

3. Seventy-two-inch round tables (six feet) can seat 10 comfortably and 12 in a tight squeeze. The less common 60" table (five feet) seats eight comfortably and can accommodate up to 10 people.

A+ meeting specifications

Normally about three or four weeks prior to your meeting, you'll give the venue a compiled document giving very specific information about each function. My colleagues and I call these meeting specifications. I've also heard the term "function resume." The hotel will use your specifications to fill in their banquet event orders (BEOs), which are distributed to every department so that they can see the role they're playing in your meeting. (The BEOs are sent to you first for your review, approval, and signature, before they are distributed to the hotel staff.) Figure 6.3 shows actual meeting specifications for a series of meetings and events that were held in conjunction with a trade show. The specifications you send to your CSM will be complete — that is, you'll provide specifications for each function (Figure 6.3 is only a sampling).

Figure 6.3

Date

[CSM's name]
Four Seasons Hotel
121 E. Delaware Place
Chicago, IL 60611

Dear [CSM's name]:

This letter and attachments will confirm and outline the WIDGET ASSOCIATION's requirements for our functions being held at your hotel October 7–11.

WIDGET ASSOCIATION has arranged a direct bill master account with your hotel for the following charges:

      * Banquet Food & Beverage Functions

      * Meeting Room Equipment

      * WIDGET ASSOCIATION Sleeping Room, Tax, and Incidentals for those individuals noted on our rooming lists

Fern Dickey, CMP, WIDGET ASSOCIATION's Director of Widget Education, will be responsible for working with the hotel and signing for all food and beverage functions. I'd like to ask that you meet with me on Friday morning, October 6, at 9:00 a.m. in order to review the specifications for the week and check the suite for Mr. Chairman of the Board, who will be arriving that day.

I'd also like to check Mr. Association President's room, as well. Please let me know if this will be a problem.

Attached is a complete specification for the meeting room and food/beverage functions that we will require.

I look forward to speaking with you upon receipt of this letter. Thank you for your excellent service.

Sincerely,

Fern Dickey, CMP

Director, Widget Education

Enclosures

WIDGET ASSOCIATION Specifications [Partial]

Thursday, October 5

Time:	9:30 p.m. (approximate)
Event:	Arrival of F. Dickey

Friday, October 6

Function #2

Time:	11:00 a.m.
Event:	Chairman Suite Bar Set-up
Location:	Suite 4601
Set-up:	Please set full bar with deluxe brands
Covers:	20 people
F & B:	Dry snacks to be placed around the living area of the suite. (Potato chips, peanuts, pretzels, etc.)
Misc.:	Place two flower arrangements in the suite. One in the living area and one in the bedroom. Please spend $75 for each arrangement.

Special attention needs to be addressed to this function. Mr. Chairman would like to have the bar set upon his arrival at the hotel. He would also like to have the bar refreshed twice daily. Please check with Mrs. Chairman on other needs she may have. We can discuss on Friday morning.

Saturday, October 7

Function #1

Time: 9:30 a.m.–noon

Event: Executive Committee Meeting

Location: Oak Room

Set-up: U-shape

Covers: 13 people

F & B: We'd like the following on a Buffet Table at the back of the meeting room:

* Coffee, Tea, Decaf

A/V: One overhead projector

One screen

Audio taping equipment with blank tapes

Please have room set and ready by 7:00 a.m. Also, please allow plenty of space between each person. We'd like no more than two people at each six-foot table.

Note: There will be a break from approximately 10:15–10:30 a.m. Coffee can be refreshed at this time.

Function #2

Time: 6:00–8:00 p.m.

Event: Chairman's Reception

Location: Would like Suite 4601. Is it large enough?

Set-up: Cocktail rounds with plenty of chairs.

Covers: 75–100

F&B: Full open bar with premium brands.

Cheese display with fruit, crackers, and breads.

Vegetable display with assorted dips.

Hot hors d'oeuvres: mini pizzas, grilled chicken brochettes.

Can the chef make other suggestions for food?

Conclusion

Quick steps

1. Work closely with your CSM while you're planning your event.
2. Keep in contact with the reservations department so you can track room pick up.
3. Give the hotel clear, concisespecifications for your meeting.

Quick tips

- ⊕ Negotiate complimentary setups for rooms and for A/V equipment.
- ⊕ Review your program format with the CSM before you flesh it out.
- ⊕ Put everything in writing.

Chapter 7

Communicating with Attendees

O nce an attendee has chosen your event, make it as easy as possible for him to understand exactly what to expect. Also make it easy for him to respond and register; make his travel plans to get to your event; and navigate once on site.

The nuts and bolts of communicating with attendees

Brochure and registration form

For conferences and events, you'll have a brochure or invitation with a registration form. Make the registration form simple to read, understand, fill out, and return. That's your goal.

Space won't permit reprinting an entire brochure here, so I've listed the elements that should be included. There's no need to reinvent the wheel here. Collect conference brochures you receive and see the wording for each of these sections. Adapt the ones you like to your own brochures.

Cover page:

- ☼ Title of the program.
- ☼ Dates.
- ☼ Location.
- ☼ Key reason to attend.

(Note: It is amazing how many brochures I get where this information is buried on other pages.)

Inside pages:

- ☼ Objectives (who should attend — and why).
- ☼ Short overview about the importance of the event's topic or theme.
- ☼ Program schedule "at a glance" (dates and times of sessions listed on a page or two). This includes the titles of sessions followed by description copy. If possible, add bullets about what will be learned during the session. Sometimes it is appropriate to add level of knowledge (for example, "for entry level sales people" or "for sales people with three to five years of experience in the field").
- ☼ Speakers' names and bios.
- ☼ Advisory committee.
- ☼ Special events, such as spouse programs and tours, golf tournaments, banquets, and so forth.
- ☼ Sponsors.
- ☼ Exhibitors.
- ☼ General information (not all of these will apply for every event):

- Registration procedures.
- Accommodations.
- Recommended dress.
- Airline discounts (if you've arranged deals with certain airlines).
- Airport transfer.
- Car rentals.
- Babysitting/childcare services.
- Registration desk hours.
- Continuing education credits.
- Fees and à la carte pricing (Detail what's included in the registration fee. For example, you could simply say: "Registration includes attendance at all general sessionsand your choice of breakout sessions on Monday and Tuesday; continental breakfast each morning; refreshment breaks each day; and luncheons on Monday and Tuesday." This clarifies for attendees which meals will be on their own, and which events — such as preconference workshops — cost extra.)
- Cancellation/refund policies.

- Registration Form (can include, but is not limited to):
  - Attendee information (name, title, company).
  - Spouse/guest information.
  - Conference registration. If there are concurrent or fee-based additional sessions, they will be listed with a space to check off next to the sessions the attendees plan to attend. You'll use this information to control room counts. (You do this so that you

don't exceed the maximum seating capacity ofthe meeting room. You may have to close sessions or special events once they fill up. Start a waiting list. Let people know that space for some sessions is limited on the registration form and advise them to register early.)

- 🕐 Fee for each category of registrant (member vs. nonmember, early bird, and so forth).
- 🕐 Payment method.
- 🕐 Deadline dates.
- 🕐 Cancellation and refund policy.
- 🕐 Information on special needs of attendees with regard to the ADA and diet. Note that including information regarding the ADA is mandatory. Here is sample information you can include: For ADA compliance: "Please indicate here if you need auxiliary aids or services as identified in the Americans with Disabilities Act and we will contact you." For dietary needs: "Please check if you have special dietary needs and we will call you."
- 🕐 On-site registration desk location and hours.

Back page:

If it is a self-mailer, a portion of it is designed for mailing (return address, indicia, and so forth). Depending on how much space is left, add copy that highlights something special and exciting—the location, a keynote speaker, a new product unveiling, anything noteworthy.

As with catalogs you receive in the mail, every page of the brochure should have a phone number the reader can call if they have questions. It's even better if you can add a contact name next to that phone number. For example: "Questions? Call Fern Dickey at [PHONE NUMBER]."

Confirmation of registration

Registrations should be acknowledged with a follow-up, mailed within a week of processing the registration. The purpose of the confirmation notice is to let the attendee know that he is all set for the upcoming program. A quick turnaround on this will give the attendee confidence in the professionalism of the program. Plus, you don't want to be bombarded with calls from people wondering if they are indeed registered for the program.

Your confirmation letter should thank the attendee for choosing your program and inform him of important details (this can eliminate last minute requests for this information). Confirmation notices vary in length and in degree of detail of information. Figure 7.1 is a sample confirmation for an annual executive conference.

Figure 7.1

Dear Widget Conference Registrant:

Thank you for registering for the Widget Conference at the Four Seasons Biltmore Hotel, Santa Barbara, California from February 17–20. We are looking forward to a cutting-edge educational event and are excited that you will be a part of it. Enclosed is a copy of your conference acknowledgment. **Please review carefully.**

Acknowledgments: Please review the attached registration acknowledgment, making any necessary changes on the acknowledgment and faxing those changes to [FAX NUMBER] at your earliest convenience. We'd like to keep on-site additions/deletions to a minimum, as some activities may not be available at the last minute.

Dress: Casual business attire, khakis, polo-type shirts or button down shirts, blazers, and sweaters are the order of the day except for the awards banquet. Please bring a sweater or jacket to the meeting rooms, as meeting room temperatures and personal comfort ranges vary widely. Business attire is appropriate for the Widget Awards cocktail hour and banquet.

Hotel: The cutoff date for our room block is January 22, 2000. Please make your reservations, if you haven't already, to ensure your place. Remember to mention you're with the Widget Association to get our special room rate.

Widget Awards Dinner: Please make sure your meal selection is noted on the acknowledgment. If not, please note this information on your acknowledgment and fax it to [FAX NUMBER].

Outstanding Balances: As noted in the brochure, all balance must be submitted by February 4.

Refund Policy: Cancellations received on or before [DATE] entitle you to a full refund. Cancellations received after [DATE] will be assessed a $200 administrative charge. You may substitute colleagues from the same company at no additional charge. Cancellations must be made in writing. No shows, without written or faxed notice prior to the conference, are responsible for payment in full.

Directions: Directions from Santa Barbara and Los Angeles International airports are enclosed

Santa Barbara Dine-Around: As part of your on-site packet you will receive an Official Visitor's Guide to help you enjoy your stay in Santa Barbara and to use in selecting your restaurant choice for Friday night's dine-around.

Weather: Sunny and warm.

Mid-February high temperature range: 68–72 degrees

Mid-February low temperature range: 59–63 degrees

Bring sunscreen, but also bring an umbrella – just in case.

On-site Registration: Our registration desk will be located in the [LOCATION]. Please stop by [DATE and TIME] to pick up your name badge and conference packet. We have some special goodies for spouses and guests as well.

Our first get together will be the Chairman's Welcome Reception on Wednesday, February 17, at 6:00 p.m. A full conference schedule with room locations will be in your on-site registration packet.

If you need auxiliary aids or services as identified in the Americans with

Disabilities Act, please call me at [PHONE NUMBER].

See you in Santa Barbara,

Fern Dickey

Widget Conference Director

P.S. Attendees are going to receive a two-inch binder of conference material. Please leave room in your suitcase or arrange for shipping at the Four Seasons' business center.

Include the attendee's final acknowledgment/invoice with this letter. The acknowledgment should list the conference fee, the sessions and activities he signed up for (and costs), his meal selection for special food functions, deposits paid, and any balance owed. Also include a copy of your listing of his reservation, if you are handling attendees' registration, so he can confirm his itinerary.

Customer service

Attendees will call your staff with questions ranging from the logical to the bizarre. Take the time to train your staff to answer them. Your staff members need to learn how to provide answers and maintain their cool and sense of humor. Your conversations with attendees and potential attendees are an opportunity to show that your organization produces the most well-run and well-organized events and that your organization's staff is first-class.

Travel arrangements

It will be easiest for you to have attendees make their own travel arrangements. You may want to provide them with some travel tips, though. If you have the budget to do so, a worthwhile (and inexpensive at 25 cents per copy) booklet from the Professional Convention Management Association (877-827-7262) called *Enjoy Your Meeting Safely* is filled with tips about hotel safety, transportation safety, fire precautions, and emergency measures.

An interesting Internet service called b-there.com, located in Westport, Connecticut (*www.b-there.com*; 877-828-4373), provides what it calls "Internet Attendee Relationship Management" (ARM). ARM provides an array of online tools to enable event attendees to do things from registering for all of their sessions to purchasing airline tickets at event-specific negotiated airfares, to researching their destination, reserving tickets, or making restaurant reservations. To make the service available to your attendees, you simply have to register your event with b-there.com. These types of services are still new and fairly untested. Meeting planners and attendees will both benefit as these types of services become standard operating procedure.

On-site communications

Registration packets

You (or someone you appoint) will be putting together on-site registration packets for attendees. At the very minimum, the packet will contain a name badge and a conference schedule. Packets vary program to program. They are good vehicles to promote excitement about the event via small gifts or surprises and can be used to promote your organization and your products and services. Figure 7.2 is a sample list of materials that went into the registration packets at a major conference. Note that there were two types of packets assembled: one for attendees and one for their spouses and guests.

Tip: Even if you've mailed your attendees schedules and other information they'd need on site, many will leave it at home, so it's best to plan to give them another copy on site.

Figure 7.2

Widget Symposium
On-Site Handout Packets

ATTENDEES

1. Personalized Envelope Packet containing:
    - Name badge.
    - Welcome letter.
    - Golf and/or tennis info.
    - Ribbons (These stick on name badges and identify people as attendees, staff, speakers, press, and so on.)

2. Canvas bag with Widget Association logo containing:
    - Notebooks, which contain:
        - Letter from Education Chairman.
        - Handout material.
    - Conference pen.
    - Promotional postcard for next year's event.
    - Attendee list.
    - Speaker list (with bios).
    - Staff list.
    - Daily Program Schedule and map of Four Seasons floor plan.
    - Visitors' guide to Santa Barbara.

SPOUSES/GUESTS

1. Plastic handle bags with Widget logo
    - Daily Schedule and map of Four Seasons' floor plan.
    - Gift (fanny pack).
    - Sponsor gift (clock).
    - List of spouse events with welcome letter from Chairman of the Board's spouse.
    - Visitor's guide to Santa Barbara.

Let's talk now about a few of the elements in the registration packet.

Welcome letters are a warm way to greet attendees. You can include program changes or bring their attention to important details in such a letter. Figure 7.3 is a welcome letter from a conference held on Northwestern University's college campus.

Figure 7.3

MEMO

TO: Widget Institute Attendees
FROM: Fern Dickey
RE: Misc.
DATE: June 11

Welcome to this year's Widget Institute. Some information to know. . .

GETTING TO CLASS AT THE NORRIS CENTER. We've given you maps, but the easiest thing to do if you're a first-timer is to join the group for breakfast here at the Omni Hotel and then walk together to the Norris Center. If you're running late, ask the front desk for walking directions (or you can always take a cab!)

(Classes are at Northwestern University's Norris University Center, 1999 South Campus Drive, 847-491-2300.)

We've arranged for our Widget Institute attendees to utilize Northwestern University's **Sport/Aquatic Center** on the Northwestern Campus for $8 per visit. For information and hours, please call 491-2300.

Throughout the next five days, you'll be seeing lots of EVALUATION FORMS. There's one for each instructor and an overall one for the course itself. They really don't take long to fill out and help us continue to bring quality education to the industry. Your comments and insights mean a great deal to NAPL. Please bear with us.

WIDGET INSTITUTE TRIVIA BOWL is a new addition to our Widget Institute. The first annual Trivia Bowl will take place in the Omni's Grand Ballroom

Monday, June 14. It will be played like TV's *Jeopardy!* game show. Wine, beer, soda, and light refreshments will be served. Your instructors will fill you in on the details. Please join us Monday before you head out to dinner.

GRADUATION is scheduled for **Wednesday, June 16, from 11:30 a.m. until noon** in McCormick Auditorium at the Norris Center.

If you need help, or just want to chat, the following Widget Association staff are on site all week:

John President, President
Gale Vip, Vice President
Fern Dickey, Director, Widget Education

Have a wonderful week!

Best Regards,

Fern

🕐🕐🕐

    A daily agenda is a very important document. Figure 7.4 is a sample of one day's agenda from a four-day conference to give you an idea of the information to include. Tip: In addition to stuffing these into registration packets, keep a large supply at your registration desk. People tend to misplace them throughout the event.

Figure 7.4

1999 Widget Engineers Annual Conference
Daily Program Schedule

Thursday, February 18

8:00a.m.–11:00 p.m.	**Hospitality Suite**	Odell Cottage
7:30–8:30 a.m.	Opening Breakfast	La Bella Vista
8:15–8:45 a.m.	Refreshment Break	Loggia Terrace
8:45 a.m.–Noon	General Session	Loggia Ballroom
9:00–10:30 a.m.	"Get Acquainted" Spouse/ Guest Breakfast	La Marina
10:15–10:30 a.m.	General Session Refreshment Break	Loggia Terrace
10:30–10:45 a.m.	Presentation of Industry Award	Loggia Ballroom
11:30a.m.–4:00 p.m.	Tour: "Lotusland Garden Tour"	Off-Site

(11:15 a.m..–Bus arrives for Lotusland Tour at Grand Entrance.)

1:00–1:45 p.m.	Refreshment Break	North Patio
1:00–5:00 p.m.	Golf Tournament	Sandpiper Golf Course
1:30–3:00 p.m.	**Breakout Sessions**	
	"Customers as Production Partners"	Las Flores/El Pres
	"Widget Technology"	El Jardin/La Loma
	"Widget Workflows"	El Mar
7:00–10:00 p.m.	Theme Party: Disco Fever	La Pacifica/ CC Lawn

Registration desk

Because this is the hub of your program, make sure the hours are posted in several places. Use the hotel's reader board, place a sign at the registration area, and include the registration desk hours in your daily schedule.

Program wrap-up

No matter how successful the meeting, any time people have been away from home and office for a few days, they're eager to get back. You can help make that happen more smoothly if the hotel is ready with staff available to handle baggage, checkouts, and transportation. Ask the hotel concierge to alert cab companies that a large meeting will be letting out at a certain time and that people will be going to the local airports. As an alternative, ask if the hotel can arrange extra shuttles to the airport.

If you have presented awards or large items of that nature, be ready to handle last minute requests to ship them back to offices. Decide on how you'll handle this before you get on site (that is, whether you'll handle it or ask the recipient to go to the business center).

Your staff is eager to get home, as well, and may be busy packing up the registration desk and other things. Ask them to stay around to help attendees. Until the last attendee is out the door, your role as the meeting manager isn't over.

Conclusion

Quick steps

1. Make sure your brochure and registration forms give attendees any and all vital information.
2. Send confirmations within one week of processing the registration.
3. Create on-site registration packets that help attendees make the most of their time at the event.

Quick tips

⊕ Important details are worth repeating. Do so in the brochure, in the confirmation, and again in the on-site material.

⊕ You're in charge of the attendees' well-being. Think of yourself as the den leader, teacher, or airline attendant. They didn't have to choose your meeting; make them glad they did.

Chapter 8

Working with Vendors

"After the verb 'to Love,' 'to Help' is the most beautiful verb in the world."
— Bertha von Suttner

T he venue can't provide every service, so you'll need to turn to other sources for their help. These include catering (when you're at a special venue, such as a museum), rentals (tents, chairs, china), photography, music, transportation, audio/video taping, "back of the room" resale, and temporary help. In fact, according to *Agenda New York* magazine, rentals often account for a third of the total expense of the event.

If your meeting isn't local, the best way to find vendors is to ask your contact at the venue for referrals. However, don't assume that the recommended service provider will be less expensive because of its connection with the venue. You can also ask the area's CVB or chamber of commerce.

Three terrific online vendor directories are:

1. ASAE's buyer's guide (*www.asaenet.org*), which provides searchable directories of associations and association suppliers.

2. *Successful Meetings* magazine's Web site (*www.successmtg.com*), which has a comprehensive directory of services.

3. Plansoft.com (*www.plansoft.com*), which has a directory with more than 30,000 suppliers.

The big guns

Three major pieces of your meeting that may be outsourced are destination management, registration, and housing. They're often outsourced because they're time-consuming, hard to do without experience, and so darned important to the outcome of your event. Additionally, registration can be exceedingly complex if the event has a lot of activities, and it might be impossible to handle registration without specialized software.

Destination management companies (DMCs)

If you've got to plan extracurricular activities for your meeting, budget to hire a DMC. These companies create special events and spouse programs, tours, golf tournaments, and other sport activities; develop theme parties and hire entertainment; coordinate off-site events; and handle attendees' transportation once they reach the destination's airports and train stations.

The CVB and the venue will refer you to local DMCs, but you can also contact the Association of Destination Management Executives, headquartered in Denver, Colorado (*www.adme.org*; 303-394-3905), to research its listing of more than 1,000 destination management executives.

Registration

Attendees will sign up for your event during one of two registration periods: advance or on site.

Advance registration. Most people will register in advance. If your meeting is simple and small (less than 100 people) you may want to handle it yourself — using Microsoft Word, Microsoft Excel, or some other software program. You can also buy meeting management software, which can cost anywhere from hundreds of dollars to thousands of dollars. (This may be worth investigating if you'll be planning a lot of meetings in the future.)

If you expect a large turnout and are planning a lot of on-site activities, you'd be wise to outsource registration.

There are many registration management companies, and now there are options to handle this process via the Web. Here are some well-known registration solution providers:

1. Conferon is the largest meeting planning firm in the United States. Some of the services it offers include meeting planning, site selection, hotel contract negotiating, registration, housing, and trade show sales/management. It offers Web-based registration along with the more traditional mail, phone, and fax methods. Conferon is headquartered in Cleveland, Ohio, and has regional sales offices as well. (*www.conferon.com*; 330-425-8333)

2. Passkey.com, based in Quincy, Mass., provides help with housing, registration, and travel. According to its Web site, it is the only meeting planner resource that hosts a live group reservation system, accessible 24 hours a day, seven days a week. (*www.passkey.com*; 800-211-4234)

3. Momentix, located in Boston, Mass., offers an online registration management system with integrated registration for attendees, speakers, exhibitors and vendors; secure online credit card processing; registration management and administration; invoicing; and badge printing. (*www.momentix.com*; 617-338-5165)

4. SeeUthere.com, located in Mountain View, Calif., a partner of the well-known PlanSoft company, can also help with the registration process by sending invitations via e-mail, mail, and fax; offering guest registration via the Web and telephone; and tracking RSVPs online. (*www.seeUthere.com*; 650-947-1800)

5. Event411, based in Marina del Ray, Calif., was one of the first online planning companies and remains one of the largest. It offers complete online event planning. (*www.event411.com*; 310-574-9000)

6. B-there.com, in Westport, Conn., is an online registration and reservation system that lets attendees register for sessions, book hotels, and purchase airline tickets at event-specific negotiated airfares, among other services. (*www.b-there.com*; 877-828-4373).

All of these companies will handle the entire registration process, including setting up registration forms, collecting payments, sending confirmations to attendees, producing registration activity reports, generating name badges, and sometimes even doing a marketing analysis of attendees for you. Most of these companies will handle housing management, air and ground transportation, and destination information as well.

On-site registration. Two things happen during on-site registration. The majority of people will have already registered in advance and will just be "checking in" on site. They'll come to your registration area to check-in, pick up their name badge, and get their conference/meeting material. Depending on your activities, they may also have to go to the registration desk to sign up for activities or to exchange meal tickets for banquet functions. A small number of people, perhaps 15 percent, will be walk-ins. That means they'll be registering for the event on site. You'll need to get their information (name, address, and so forth), sign them up for activities, collect payment, make a name badge, and prepare a packet of on-site material for them.

At most events, you'll set up a registration area. The registration area can be likened to your kitchen when you're hosting a party. Everyone hangs out there; it's the meet-and-greet place. If your meeting is simple, small, and/or consists of one event held in one room, your registration area might be a six-foot table set up right outside the meeting room laid out with name badges and welcome packets. For larger meetings, you'll be set up in a main area or hallway; either with several tables forming a U-shape or at an actual space the venue has specifically designed for registration.

In staffing your on-site registration area, plan to have one registration person per 100 attendees. If you can have two per 100, that's even better. That way, you can have one person handle the registration process and one person handle the "problems" that inevitably occur (misspelled name badges, missing registration packets, etc.). You can hire experienced registration people through the Convention & Visitors Bureau or through independent companies such as Conferon or Meeting In-Site in Hoboken, N.J. (*www.meetinginsite.com*; 201-420-6878).

Housing

If you don't have the time or the expertise to manage housing, one very popular option is to require your attendees make their own reservations. However, as with registrations, if you have a large group, you should look into contracting a housing company to manage your needs. Regardless of who makes reservations, be sure to keep track of the rooms being booked; you may have special requirements written into your hotel contract (such as upgrades for your executive board or a complimentary room for every 40 rooms booked), and you'll want to monitor attendance. Most of the registration companies listed in the previous section can handle housing, and your CVB is a great source for housing help.

Other vendors

This list highlights other commonly hired services and vendors.

Caterers

You'll need to hire a caterer if your event isn't at a hotel or a restaurant. Venues without on-site catering will have a list of caterers that they work with — sometimes exclusively, which means you will be required to use someone on their list. Other venues can provide suggestions, as can the CVB or a DMC. A great source for fine caterers in the major cities in the U.S. is *www.agendaonline.com.* There are all kinds of caterers specializing in all kinds of needs, styles, and budgets. When you are selecting a caterer, ask to see menus, a list of clients, and price lists, and, as always, ask for (and call) references. If your event is local, you may ask the caterer for a tasting and to see them handle an event.

When working with a caterer, you'll review menus, equipment rental (you may need tables and chairs, china, bars, and so forth, as each venue has different equipment on hand), and staffing requirements. Make sure you get everything you've agreed upon in writing. Two things you must have included in the contract are the caterer's state health license and its liability insurance. Make sure the contract mentions all possible fees, including gratuities and costs if more people than expected show up. (Find out how the caterer handles this so you know if you'll have to turn people away; see Chapter 6 for monitoring attendance at meal functions.)

Transportation

You'll need to address three areas as far as transportation is concerned:

1. Transportation of attendees to and from the airport. Many hotels offer complimentary shuttle service to and from nearby airports, but they often need advance notice of arrivals and departures. Taxis are also an option, as are limousine or bus services and car rental agencies. You can offer all these options to attendees and require them to arrange their own transportation. The nicest way to do this is to list phone numbers of transportation services in your promotional material so that all the attendees have to do is pick up the telephone.

2. Transportation of all or part of the group to any off-site events. You can be creative when you're transporting a group around a city. In addition to the usual cabs and limousines, you can charter buses, trolleys, or watercrafts. We once surprised an executive board of directors by transporting them to a trade show via trolley after their meeting. It was fun and different, and it gave them an opportunity to stay together and continue their conversations.

3. Special transportation for VIPs. The VIPs' first impression of your meeting will be the welcome they receive at the airport. Putting together a chart for your vendor of who's arriving when and on what airline will help make this important task flow more smoothly. If you can't meet with your transportation vendor, then use the tips below to make sure you're hiring the right quality for your group.

Tips include:

- Get a list of the types of vehicles in the vendor's inventory.
- Find out the condition and age of all vehicles.
- Make sure the vehicles are compliant with the Americans with Disabilities Act (ADA).
- Understand minimum hours and costs.
- Make sure the vendor is properly insured by asking for a certificate of insurance.
- Have a contact person who will be available to you 24 hours a day during your meeting.
- Make sure the vendor provides a written contingency plan for all your transportation orders.
- Find out what duties the driver/operator will perform (for example, have a sign with the VIP's name, get and carry the luggage from the baggage claim area, park close to the baggage area so that the VIP won't have to walk a long distance, etc.).

Security

Most hotels have a security staff for general safety purposes. Some situations require hiring and/or using additional security staff. You might have an exhibit area that needs to be secured during off-hours, or you may have a celebrity speaker that requires protection. If that's the case, work with a company that caters to the meetings industry rather than a general business security firm.

Temporary help

Many times you'll need helping hands — whether it be stuffing registration packets, handling the registration desk, manning a book sales booth, or helping you oversee your sessions. You can ask the CVB for a list of temp agencies with experience in the meetings industry. Be specific about what you need in terms of hours, responsibilities, skill, and demeanor.

It's helpful to make a chart listing the days and times you'll need staff, how many staff people per each time period, what they'll be doing, and where they're to be. Figure 8.1 is a simple temporary staffing chart.

Figure 8.1

Temporary Registration Personnel
1999 Widget Conference
June 10–16, 1999
Omni Orrington Hotel/Northwestern University
Evanston, Illinois

Day/ Date	No. of People	Hours	Responsibilities	Location
Thurs. June 10	2	10 a.m–5 p.m.	Orientation, unpacking boxes, stuffing registration packets, setting up and manning registration desk. (Organizing badges, signs, handout materials.)	Omni Orrington (Lunt Room)
Fri. June 11	2	9 a.m.–5 p.m.	Stuffing registration packets, helping with registration set up. Move meeting materials from hotel to university via van provided by hotel. Set up classrooms at Norris Center with binders and notepads. Set up "books for sale" table and office area.	Omni Orrington Hotel and Norris Center at Northwestern Univ.
Sat. June 12 through Tues. June 15	1	8 a.m.–4 p.m.	Help instructors with copying, running errands, assisting students. Man sales booth during breaks. Some light typing and office work.	Norris Center at Northwestern Univ.
Wed. June 16	1	8 a.m.–Noon	Help pack up office supplies for shipping back to headquarters. Set up graduation ceremony.	Norris Center at Northwestern Univ.

Need: intelligent, well-spoken, experienced people who are comfortable with being left alone at registration desk.

Florists

Flowers are expensive, but they really can make a dramatic difference in the ambiance of an event. If your budget is limited, you can make the most out of less expensive arrangements by combining them with candles, glass objects, or other centerpieces. One important tip I learned the hard way: If you're planning to use flowers during a meal event, make sure their odor is not too pervasive! You'll find local florists the same way you'll find the other vendors. Use the same care in selection by checking references and asking to see pictures of their work.

Bands

Music can transform your event, whether it be a single piano player, a jazz trio, or a seven-piece band. Get referrals and lists from the venue, the CVB, and the chamber of commerce. You can also use a music broker to find just the right musical group for your event, if the music is the keystone for the program.

Here are some selection tips:

1. Ask for sample tapes.
2. Have several people from your organization listen to the tapes (together if possible.)
3. Ask for the band's song list. (You can use this list to tell them what *not* to play!)

To make the evening flow smoothly, make sure the band has information about your group, your evening's agenda, and who they will need to talk to at the venue about set up very early in advance. As the date draws closer, make sure the band has directions, the correct place to unload its equipment, a convenient place to park, the venue's contact person and phone number, and refreshments provided during breaks as appropriate.

As with all other vendor contracts, put the basics in writing: the date, time, place, style of music, and budget. With all vendors, make sure you have also listed what time the musicians will arrive so you won't panic about them not showing up! The contract should list the number of personnel you've agreed to, their attire, their schedule of breaks (to complement your schedule of course) the style of music, the fees (including overtime), setup and rehearsal (if any) requirements, and any special needs.

Photographers

Make sure you're hiring the right type of photographer for your event. In my early days, I hired a very lovely woman to take pictures at an educational event held on a college campus. I didn't realize she specialized in artistic photography rather than event photography, and I ended up with a few usable pictures of my attendees and lots of wonderful shots of the campus that should have been made into posters. The lesson? Review samples/portfolios from prospective photographers' work and call their references.

Besides referrals from the CVB and the venue, you can search further through two good sources. The American Society of Media Photographers in Philadelphia, PA (*www.asmp.org*; 215-451-2767) has been around for more than 50 years, is internationally recognized, and has more than 5,000 U.S. members, including many of the world's greatest photographers. The other source is Primeshot.com (*www.primeshot.com*; 703-469-3821), headquartered in Washington, D.C., which enables you to book professional photographers online and even allows your attendees to view and share the event pictures in password-protected galleries and then purchase Kodak-paper prints and related items.

Because you may be paying by the hour, careful planning will save you money. Here are some tips.

1. Find out who in your organization needs or wants photos of the event.

2. Are these other parties going to split the charges with you? (If so, put it in writing!)

3. Make a draft schedule for the photographer. Run it by everyone involved. Review it yourself. Think about what you need and when that might happen. For example, if you are taking pictures of a trade show booth, do you need pictures of it empty for historical purposes and then pictures of it filled with people for later publicity needs? (If so, ask the photographer to show up at least a half hour before the show opens and then to stay when attendees are admitted.) Think also about special events such as awards ceremonies, which usually require "live" shots of the person(s) receiving the award as well as staged "grip and grin" shots of the awardee surrounded by, say, your executive staff.

4. Try to minimize the time the photographer needs to be on site for you. The photographer will have minimum hours that you'll have to consider, but there's no need for him to hang out all day at your golf tournament and take an untold number of rolls of film if you're just going to use one or two shots for a brochure.

5. Decide if you want proof sheets or 4x6 proofs. Get pricing for both from the photographer. (I prefer 4x6 proofs, because the ones we don't use can be mailed to attendees and speakers in their thank-you letters.

6. Decide if your pictures will be in color or black and white. (Digital photography may be an option for you as well.)

Working with vendors

1. Make sure you have a 24-hour phone number for emergencies.
2. Call each vendor two weeks before your event and again the day before to confirm arrangements.
3. Keep track of deposits and payments. Each vendor will require a deposit and then a balance due, which is usually due on site and not after the event ends.
4. If you can't afford the first rates offered to you, don't despair. Be fair, be honest, and ask for the rates you can afford. That's your best bargaining tool.
5. Get it in writing. There must be a written agreement outlining everything the vendor has agreed to do for your event. Review it for accuracy and run it by your legal counsel.
6. Communicate often with your vendors. Sharing information such as promotional brochures, invitations, and press releases will help the vendor understand your group and the purpose of your event.

Conclusion

Quick steps

1. Review your vendor needs.
2. Plan a budget.

3. Select the vendors.

4. Negotiate and sign a contract with each vendor.

Quick tips

☺ Let the venue and the CVB help you find vendors.

☺ If the price the vendor quotes is too high, ask for the price you need.

Chapter 9

Legal Issues

"A verbal contract isn't worth the paper it's written on."
—Goldwyn's Law of Contracts

All events require contracts and insurance policies. The contracts outline and explain responsibilities; commitments and agreements; and processes, terms, and conditions. Venue contracts are the most complex, but you'll have contracts or letters of agreement with everyone you work with outside of your own organization.

Insurance, technically, is a type of contract that guarantees another party against loss by a specified contingency or danger. There will be different types of insurance depending on the event, the most common being cancellation insurance, commercial general liability, and liquor (or "host") liability.

Your role is to review all contracts to make sure that the information and terms you agreed to are

129

stated correctly. You should have legal counsel review and advise on contracts; they can also negotiate on your behalf. Ask your company's insurance agent to advise on insurance needs and policies.

Contracts

Although I can't dispense any legal advice, I can give you a primer on some common contractual clauses in the meeting and event industry. In recent years, hotel contracts in particular have become long, cumbersome documents detailing more than 90-plus clauses. They can range from a two- or three-page contract for a small meeting to a document of 25 or more pages.

Unless you are an executive of your organization, you should absolutely not sign contracts. Check with your top brass and your accounting department to find out who has the authority to sign contracts. If you sign, you can be held personally liable if any misfortune occurs.

Venue contracts

Meeting industry legal expert John S. Foster said at a recent seminar, "Clarify[ing] at the front end saves you from begging at the back end." What he means is that you should be clear and concise and make sure every contingency is thought through and spelled out in the contract. He also listed the six objectives of these now-lengthy hotel agreements:

1. Clearly specify prices and rates.
    (For sleeping rooms, services such as porters and food and beverage, and meeting room rates.)
2. Specify intent and expectations.
3. Establish and list deadlines.

(This outlines the schedule for deposits, the release of sleeping rooms back into the general pool, and opportunities to reduce your sleeping room block.)

4. Allocate liability between the parties.
5. Specify remedies for breach or default.
6. Make contract legally clear, precise and inclusive.

Figure 9.1 is an outline of a comprehensive checklist of clauses for hotel contracts compiled by Jonathan Howe, Esq., a well-known legal adviser in the meeting industry. It is reprinted with permission. (My comments on the more commonly used clauses, along with samples of actual clauses, are in italics.)

Figure 9.1

Checklist of Clauses for Hotel Contracts

I. Guest Rooms

A. Room Block

This is your commitment of how many rooms you're blocking. This is a danger area because you will be liable for unsold rooms. If there are rooms left in your room block that can't be resold by the hotel, you will pay the hotel attrition. There are different calculations used to figure the "damages." Your lawyer will put it in the contract.

In days of old, planners intentionally overbooked (to make sure they had enough rooms) and hotels rarely, if ever, enforced attrition clauses. It is no longer that free and easy. You will pay attrition. And you will walk a fine line between not having enough rooms for your attendees and overbooking and paying attrition. If a meeting has no history, an educated guess along with budgeting for attrition is the best anyone can do.

B. Blocked Suites

This clause states if the hotel has agreed to give you specific rooms—for example, your group gets five specific suites with an ocean view and a fireplace for your VIPs.

C. Adjustment to Block

Established dates (usually two) when you can reduce your room block by a certain percentage without penalty.

D. Rooming Lists

E. Cutoff Date

This is the day when rooms you have reserved are released back into the hotel's general inventory for resale. You need to know this date when you are putting together your promotions so that you can alert attendees to register on time. After the cutoff date, your attendees will pay the regular hotel rate rather than the discounted rate you and the hotel have offered them.

F. Reservations

You'll determine whether attendees will be calling in to make their own reservations or whether you will be submitting a rooming list. For last minute meetings, it's best to opt to have the attendees call in. There are four ways for attendees to reserve rooms, and one of these will be in the contract:

1. *Attendees arrange their own room accommodations.*
2. *Attendees respond directly to the facility via reservation request card (card, form, fax, telephone, or Internet).*
3. *Attendees respond through you. You, in turn, provide a housing list to the facility.*
4. *Attendees respond to an outside housing bureau.*

G. Check-In and Check-Out

The hotel will state its times. You should use this information in your confirmation material to attendees so that they don't arrive too early and become frustrated when they have to wait for their room to be ready.

H. Room and Related Charges

The hotel will list its published, or rack, rates, which are usually substantially higher than the group rate you'll receive. You'll also see what the hotel charges for guest room tax.

I. Complimentary Rooms

It is common to receive one complimentary room for every 50 room nights you block. For a 190 room block, we'd receive three free room nights. Other complimentary rooms may be negotiated. For example, there are times when a presidential suite or additional rooms for staff can be complimentary, depending on the volume of your business.

J. Walking

Hotels, just like airlines and talk shows, overbook to ensure that they use every room/seat/bed. There are usually enough no-shows and cancellations to make it all work out. But, if one of your attendees finds that there are no rooms at the inn, the hotel will be required to pay for the guest to be transported to another hotel of equal caliber and will also be required to pay for lodging. The nuances of the Walking clause will be hammered out by your attorney, but ask that your group has sole approval on selecting who gets walked. That way, you can be sure your VIPs have rooms at the hotel.

II. Rates, Fees, and Charges

A. Guest Room Rates

These are the rate(s) you've been quoted and guaranteed.

B. Rate Caps

The maximum amount the room rate will increase per year. (This is relevant only if you are planning a meeting several years out.)

C. Staff Rooms

This is the number of rooms allotted to your staff at a rate discounted from your regular group rate.

D. Family Plan

This refers to any discounts offered to family members travelling with you.

E. Rate Applicability Pre and Post

You may try to negotiate your room rate to remain in effect a few days before and after your meeting so that attendees can extend the trip into a vacation.

F. Gratuities/Service Charges

This is the current service charge and service charge tax. They may also ask if you want to prearrange to pay gratuities for your guests. (You don't.)

G. Incidental Charges

You'll clarify whether or not you will be paying for guests' incidental charges (room service, laundry, etc.). Typically, you'll just pay for the incidentals for your organization's staff and/or VIPs.

H. Commissions

The venue should let you know if a commission to a third party vendor, such as an audiovisual company, is included in your rates.

III. Master Account

This is your tab. It will include every expense incurred at the venue that you've agreed to pay, including meal functions, audiovisual equipment, staff sleeping rooms, business center charges, and so on.

A. Establishment

Before the meeting, you'll set up a master account which will allow you to start a "tab" at the venue. The venue will send you some paperwork to fill out on behalf of your organization to get credit approval. You'll look to your accounting department to fill in most of the blanks.

B. Charges

The charges that will go to the master account (usually food and beverage, audiovisual, and sleeping rooms for staff). This clause will also list the names of the people who will be authorized to sign for any on-site orders (such as food, audiovisual, or business center services).

C. Daily Review

Here's where you make sure that the hotel's convention services person tracks you down at the end of each day and lets you review the day's bills for accuracy. It is so much easier to do that on site while it is all happening and fresh in your mind than seeing the hotel bill for the first time three weeks later back at your desk.

D. Billing

This is the manner in which you will receive the final bill (that is, with all daily invoices and guest folios (for staff, speakers, and anyone else you are paying for; not attendees) as backup).

E. Payment

These are the terms to which the hotel expects payment once you've received the final invoice.

IV. Function Space

A. Space Hold

Some areas of your meeting, such as your registration area, would take hours to put away each night and reset each morning. You need to keep those kind of spaces on a 24-hour hold.

   B. Complimentary Space/Complimentary Setup or Charges

This clause explains and sets the requirements for which you receive complimentary setups.

   C. Quiet Enjoyment

This clause states that your group is entitled to hold a meeting without jackhammering happening outside your meeting room door.

   D. Conflict Avoidance

The hotel is required to let you know if a competing group is planning to hold a meeting at the venue at the same time as you. (You'll provide the hotel with a list of your competitors.)

   E. Reassignment of Assigned Space

You'll ask the hotel not reassign you to another meeting space in the hotel without your written approval.

   F. Signs

Some hotels, usually of the Four Seasons' ilk, do not let you use your own signs outside of meeting rooms. In that case, they provide signs for you that conform to their standards of decor. However, you'll need to know this before you spend hundreds of dollars making signs.

   G. Audio/Visual

It is expected that you'll use the facility's in-house audiovisual services. Otherwise, it should be noted in the contract that you won't. This clause would release you from any charges.

   H. Final Program

This is a chart of your functions and the rooms they've been assigned to.

V. Exhibits

   A. Assigned Exhibit Space

   B. Charge

   C. Utilities

   D. Other

VI. Convention Coordination

   A. Coordinator

B. Radio Contact

This refers to using pagers, walkie-talkies, or other communications devices to keep in touch with your staff and the venue's staff. This is especially important when you're running a trade show in a huge complex.

C. Resume

These are the specifications for the convention, which is larger and more complex than a meeting or conference.

VII. Shipping and Handling

Besides listing the correct address for mailing materials to the venue, this clause would contain any fees the venue charges for storage and/or moving boxes.

VIII. Catering, Food, and Beverage

    A. Price Confirmation
    B. Food and Beverage Discount
    C. Food and Beverage Functions
    D. Taxes and Other Charges
    E. Catering Manager

IX. Post-Convention Report

The hotel is asked to submit an occupancy and revenue summary showing the total number of rooms and suites used per night, room revenue, comp rooms used, and the room types booked (single/double), and the revenue gained from your group. Aside from the food, beverage, and audiovisual charges, the hotel is also making money from hospitality suites (especially if it has an open bar), room service, and other groups that hold meetings because of yours (such as your board's annual planning meeting). This is valuable meeting "history" that you will absolutely use if and when you plan the same or similar event.

X. Alcoholic Beverages

    A. Service of Alcoholic Beverages

This states that only the venue's employees and bartenders can serve alcoholic beverages.

    B. Service Requirements

This states that the venue must request proper photo identification of anyone who is of questionable age and refuse service if the person is underage, doesn't have identification, or appears intoxicated.

C. Training

This requires that servers are trained to prevent incidents that would lead to liabilities.

D. Indemnification

This stats that the venue will not hold you liable against any losses, damages, claims, or liabilities caused by them serving alcoholic beverages.

XI. Duties, Responsibilities, Representations, and Warranties of the Hotel

   A. Prompt Check-In and Check-Out
   B. Safety and Health Codes Compliance
   C. Quality of the Hotel
   D. Americans with Disabilities Act Compliance
       1. Compliance
       2. Representation
       3. Identification of Needs

XII. Insurance

According to the editors of Agenda New York *magazine, "The most likely targets of lawsuits...are the caterer, the facility, and the person giving the party." Some typical policies include:*

   1. **Convention liability insurance.** *This policy covers the meeting sponsor for any unexpected expenses from legal action due to personal injury or property damage.*

   2. **Cancellation insurance.** *This policy is secured both by the venue and the meeting sponsor to provide compensation for income lost due to the cancellation of the event.*

   3. **Meeting manager's professional liability insurance.** *This policy protects the planner against claims for loss, injury, or damage if a suit extends beyond naming the organization, vendor, or facility liable.*

   A. Yours
   B. Theirs
   C. Minimums

XIII. Indemnification

Both parties agree to indemnify, defend, and hold harmless the other party (and all its members) "from and against any and all demands, claims, damages to persons or property, losses and liabilities, including reasonable attorney fees arising solely out of or caused by the indemnifying party's negligence or willful misconduct in connection with the provision and use of the facility as contemplated by this agreement."

    A. Obligation of the Hotel
    B. Obligation of the Organization

XIV. Rights of Cancellation

    A. Cancellation Generally
    B. Force Majeure

The law automatically excuses a party from performance if circumstances beyond its control prevent it from performing. Do not expand Act of God clauses to include vague or subjective terms, such as "inadvisable" or "threats of terrorism," which can lead to disputes.

    C. With Sufficient Advance Notice
    D. Financial Difficulties
    E. Deterioration in Quality

The hotel has to maintain the ratings it had when you signed the contract.

    F. Construction or Renovation

The hotel has to alert you to upcoming construction or renovation, and you have the right to cancel if you think it's going to negatively impact your meeting. You may also negotiate to have the hotel hold off on the construction, depending on what it is, until your meeting ends.

    G. Strike or other Labor Dispute
    H. Change in Management/Ownership
    I. Dependency on Others
    J. Alternate Facilities
    K. Refund Included

XV. Cancellation Fee

    A. Assessment of Fee
    B. Calculation of Fee and When It's Due
    C. Credit to Organization for Replacement Business/Future Meeting

D. Exclusivity of Remedy

XVI. Attrition

This states the penalties that your organization will pay if it doesn't meet its commitments regarding room block and food and beverage functions. The penalties often include paying for meeting space that would otherwise be complimentary.

A. Rooms
B. Meeting Space
   1. Charge
   2. Reduction
C. Food and Beverage
D. Duty to Mitigate

XVII. Breach by the Hotel

A. Rooms
B. Food and Beverage
C. Warranties

XVIII. Claims and Disputes

This is an explanation of how these would be arbitrated and resolved.

A. Litigation
B. Arbitration
C. Mediation
D. Venue
E. Choice of Law

XIX. Notices

XX. Miscellaneous

A. Section Headings
B. Modification
C. Waiver
D. Subsequent Invalidity
E. Inurement of Benefit
F. Authority to Execute

Tip: Hotel contracts are often signed by the sales manager and then mailed to you for review. You will be making changes and addendums to it. Make sure that either (a) you have the hotel's salesperson initial and date all your changes or (b) he rewrites the contract with your changes and you both sign the clean copy. The latter is recommended, especially if there are numerous changes scribbled on every page. This includes the amendments that your legal counsel will add to the initial contract.

Speaker and supplier contracts

When I contract with a speaker or vendor for its services, do I use its contract or mine? You'll use your own when hiring most speakers, unless you are working with a speakers bureau. For other vendors, you will most likely use the vendors' contracts, to which you'll negotiate, make changes, and add clauses and provisions. Use your legal counsel for review.

Other insurance packages

In addition to the packages you secure to work with the venue, here's a sampling of other type of insurance you may consider:

- ⊕ Certificate of Insurance from contractors;
- ⊕ Independent Contractors' Liability; and
- ⊕ Organization as "additional insured" for chartered transportation.

Music licensing

Most people aren't aware that most musical compositions are copyrighted intellectual property, the same way books, movies, artwork, and computer software material are. Many professional meeting planners do not know that their group is responsible for the licensing and payment of all music played at their meeting. As with using an article reprint or a chapter from a book, you need to be granted permission to use music and you need to pay for that use.

Ultimately your organization is responsible for music licensing, even if you're hiring a band to play at a function or if the hotel is providing music for you. Check with the venue, because normally it already holds a music license. If it doesn't, get in touch with one of the two major music licensing organizations. They each represent thousands of people in the music industry and protect the rights of their members by licensing and paying royalties for the public performances of their copyrighted works.

The American Society of Composers, Authors and Publishers, located in New York (*www.ascap.com*; 212-621-6000) is a membership association of more than 80,000 composers, songwriters, lyricists, and music publishers.

Broadcast Music, Inc. in Nashville, Tenn. (*www.bmi.com*; 800-925-8451), represents 250,000 songwriters, composers, and music publishers with a repertoire of more than 4.5 million compositions.

The bottom line is that you are responsible for any music played at your event. Even though the hotel may supply the music to any of the meeting or convention areas, you are responsible for licensing the music, whether it's performed live or recorded. BMI currently charges a minimum $100 annual fee based on a licensing fee of $.05 per attendee per event. The ASCAP charges a minimum annual fee of $70 at a rate of $.06 per attendee per event. You can download contracts from both organizations' Web sites. People familiar with music licensing agree that you need to contract with both organizations to "cover your bases."

Conclusion

Quick steps

1. Make sure you know who in your organization is authorized to sign contracts.
2. Read documents for accuracy of dates and other specific information.
3. Give documents to your legal counsel and insurance agents for review.
4. Have all changes and addendums on any document signed and dated by both parties.

Quick tips

- Don't be your own legal advisor or insurance agent. You must use the experts.
- Get everything in writing—and get it signed.

Chapter 10

Miscellaneous Meeting Particulars

T his chapter covers a hodgepodge of samples, tips, and explanations of meeting-related items.

Awards banquets

If you've got any kind of awards banquet, make sure you rehearse. Schedule the first rehearsal early on in case you need to schedule additional rehearsals. This may mean pulling the key players in the ceremony away from other activities, and you'll have to pay an audiovisual technician for his time, but it's worth it. The consequences of a flawed presentation are that you and your organization look bad—and that could seriously damage the tempo of the rest of the conference.

Scripts

Your conference moderators will need a script to follow. Whether you write their words for them or not, they need to know what time they're up on stage, who will be speaking before them, and who they'll be introducing when they're done. Here's a sample script from one session of a five-day annual conference.

WIDGET CONFERENCE SCRIPT
THURSDAY, FEBRUARY 18

8:45 a.m. Announcer

Welcome to the 2000 Widget Conference—the future direction of the widget industry. Please join me in welcoming Widget Association's president to the podium. A warm welcome to Mr. John President.

8:45 a.m. (President John is preparing his own opening.)

President introduces Chairman to lectern.

8:50 a.m. Chairman

Thank you, John. Welcome to Widget Association's Widget Conference. I look forward to getting to know each of you during the next few days.

We've got a phenomenal program lined up for you this week. I encourage you to take advantage of the time you'll have with your peers and our industry's experts as well as taking some time to enjoy the beauty of Santa Barbara.

I also want to extend a personal invitation for you to join us. The hospitality suite is in the Odell Cottage. It's open from 8:00 a.m. until midnight each day. Along with a terrific educational program, I believe the informal networking in the suite is one of the strongest features of the Widget Conference.

This morning's focus is on how to lead others in today's new organizational structure—and the striking differences between managing and leading.

Our speaker is the chairman and executive director of The Leadership Institute and a professor of Business Administration at USC. He's the author of more than 60 articles and five books, including his recent Winning Them Over: The New Model for Managing in the Age of Persuasion.

Mr. Jay Conger was selected by Business Week as the pick of business school professors in North America. He's an active consultant with a worldwide list of clients and an influential advisor to the business community on leadership issues. Please help me give a warm welcome to Mr. Jay Conger.

(Chairman is seated. Conger proceeds to the stage.)

9:00 a.m. Conger Presentation

Note to Mr. Congor: At 10:15, put closure to the session for the break. **Announce to the group that your session will resume in 15 minutes.**

Sponsors

Sponsorships are win-win situations. Suppliers and vendors to a pay fee, and in return they get a certain amount of recognition and exposure to your audience. Usually, you'll come up with various sponsorship levels for things including hosting breaks, meals, and keynote presentations. Golf tournaments frequently have each hole sponsored. A "platinum" sponsor might be given a chance to welcome and address attendees during a keynote session, and a "gold" sponsor could be given a full-page ad in the conference binder. Be creative. Sponsorships are a boon to your budget and in return your sponsors get their name in front of a captive target audience.

Exhibitors

There are two types of exhibits. Tabletop exhibits use six-foot or eight-foot tables to display literature and products. There can be 15 tables at a conference or symposium, or there can be 100. Exhibitors pay a fee, which covers your expenses to make signs, have tables set, have electricity brought to the tables, etc. Exhibitors also provide some revenue, though. Tabletop exhibits add excitement to an event. People can stroll around during breaks and free time, see new products and services, and chat with industry suppliers.

The second type of exhibit is a trade show. Planning a trade show is a huge undertaking and not a last minute meeting option.

On-site program guides

I personally prefer to prepare two notebooks of information for use on site: a "meeting bible" that stays at the registration desk and my own personal event guide that I have with me at all times. You may prefer to merge them.

Meeting bible

The meeting bible (also known as an event specification or staging guide) is, according to the Convention Liaison Council Manual (CLC, 1994), "a compilation of all function sheets, room setups, and other materials relevant to running the event." My event bibles contain the following tabs:

- ◷ Registrar's report (so I can see if anyone owes money and can get their balance due at registration).
- ◷ Banquet Event Orders.
- ◷ Sleeping room list.
- ◷ Function count report (a one- or two-page report listing each function with the current number of people registered).
- ◷ Acknowledgments (a list of attendees and which breakout sessions/events they are participating).

◷ Event attendance lists (a roster for every fee-based event; these are invaluable for keeping track on site of people who cancel, people who sign-up, and people who want to make substitutions).

Meeting guide

Depending on the type and size of the meeting, my guide will contain:

◷ Budget.
◷ Banquet Event Orders.
◷ Hotel contract.
◷ DMC's proposal.
◷ Golf/tennis tournaments.
◷ Hotel map.
◷ Scripts.
◷ Shipping list.
◷ Sleeping room report.
◷ Speaker grid (containing their names and phone numbers, emergency contacts, session dates/times, audiovisual requests, and arrival information).
◷ Schedules (temps/staff, speaker introductions, program and committee meetings, photography, award presentations, arrival dates/times for executive staff and VIPs).
◷ Transportation (schedules for off-site events and VIP airport transfers).
◷ Vendors (list of vendor contact information *including emergency/after-hour numbers* and vendor contracts).

VIPs

In addition to providing airport transfers and providing room upgrades, amenities are a nice welcome. Try to find out something about the VIPs and buy gifts accordingly. A chairman of one association loved cigars, so we made sure we had a good cigar waiting for him in his room, along with flowers for his spouse. Arranging for a late checkout is also a thoughtful amenity for your VIPs.

Shipping

There are certain things meeting planners will not ship, because they are too valuable to risk losing and trying to re-create. Among these things are their meeting bibles, registration materials, and anything needed immediately upon arrival. (I always ship the registration materials, because I tend to arrive on site with enough time to have our registrar reprint and reship if necessary. The registration material is too cumbersome for me to carry on board a plane.) It depends on your comfort level.

You'll create a mini-office on site. Make a list of every item (and quantity) you need to ship. Keep a list as follows (this is a *very* partial list):

QUANTITY	ITEM	BOX #
250	Badge clip holders	1
1 set	Printed tent cards (for board mtg.)	1
50	Printed session signs	2

It may seem tedious, but if you have a lot of boxes (more than 15 or 20), keep a list of the contents of each box number.

Having both lists will make it much easier to unpack and organize your on-site office, particularly when you're dealing with a room full of boxes.

Evaluations

Speaker evaluations

Especially if you have a full schedule of educational sessions, mini-evaluation forms are quick and easy to fill out. They are placed on each person's seat and filled out immediately after the session, while it's fresh in attendees' minds (as opposed to asking for comments two days later on a full two- or four-page evaluation). We get a good response rate with these little forms along with plenty of useful information. Figure 10.1 is a sample.

Figure 10.1

Widget Conference
Breakout Session Evaluation

SESSION: [TITLE OF SESSION]
SPEAKER: [SPEAKER'S NAME]
DATE: February 20

Please rate the following on a scale of 1 (poor) to 10 (excellent).

Content_____

Presentation Skills:_____

Relevance to you and/or your company_____

Comments:

I would like to learn more about:

_____

_____

Program evaluation

This is for the entire event rather than an individual speaker. There are a variety of evaluation formats you can use and questions you may want to ask. You could evaluate the educational content, the speakers, the location, and/or the extracurricular activities. You could have attendees fill out evaluations on site, or you could mail them post-meeting. Figure 10.2 is a sample of an on-site survey.

Figure 10.2

WIDGET CONFERENCE
OVERALL PROGRAM EVALUATION

1. Overall Evaluation (1 = poor; 2 = fair, 3 = good, 4 = excellent)

Overall value of educational program_____

Value to your business_____

Speakers/presentations in general_____

St. Petersburg as a conference location_____

The Renaissance Vinoy Resort_____

2a. Please list the most valuable session(s) you attended.

2b. Please list the least valuable session(s) you attended.

3. Future Planning Needs:
Please list three topics of great importance to you:

1.

2.

3.

4. Are you planning to attend next year's Widget Conference?_____

If not, please list your main reason(s):

5. Is the geographic location of the conference a primary factor in your decision to attend?_____

Please check if you would consider attending a conference in:

_____Florida   _____Bermuda

_____Arizona   _____South Carolina

_____California   _____Hawaii

_____Texas

Please list other desired location(s)

6. Please rank in order (1 = most important) the reason you attended the Conference.

Program Content_____

Peer Networking_____

Speaker Recognition_____

Location_____

7. The single most important reason I attended this meeting:

Educational_____

Networking_____

Location_____

Specific Speaker_____

Rest/Relaxation_____

Award Recognition_____

8. Comments:

Thank you. Please return to Fern Dickey or fax to [FAX NUMBER].

International meetings

You're probably not going to plan a last minute international meeting. But if you must, some of the issues you'll need to consider include:

1. Planning and programming: time differences, shipping, language barriers, insurance and contract enforcement, port of entry requirements, currency, compatibility of your equipment and their voltage, room measurements (metric vs. yards), and availability of vendors and services.
2. Translation and interpretation barriers/services.
3. Site selection: travel distance, accessibility, available transportation services, weather, holidays, and political and economic climates.
4. Local laws, customs, and etiquette.

I'd advise outsourcing to an event company with experience in international events. Start with Conferon (*www.conferon.com*; 330-425-8333) and get bids from other event planning companies.

Chapter 11

The Big Event

"We are ready for any unforeseen event that may or may not occur."
— Dan Quayle

E arly on in the planning process, you should elect someone to be the home-base contact. This person should know the same information you do (where samples of handouts are, lists of speakers, vendors, hotel contacts, how to reach you in an emergency, and so on). The home-base contact is an invaluable resource should you need something from the office relating to the event. Review the program and pertinent information before you leave the office. This person should also be someone who's willing to be available during certain hours over the weekend and have access to the office.

Plan to get to the venue between one and three days before the event, depending on the size of the meeting and how much work you've got to do on site. You and your staff have worked hard to produce your event. You're almost done—but not quite.

On-site preparation work

When you arrive at the venue, check in, call the CSM to let him know you've arrived, unpack, and then immediately check on the status of the boxes you've shipped from your office (and any you expect from vendors.) These contain the lifeblood of your event. If your boxes aren't all accounted for, you have time to have your home-base person begin tracking their location for you and make other arrangements if any boxes end up missing. After that's done, you'll probably be scheduled to meet with the hotel staff for the pre-conference meeting (known as the "pre-con").

The pre-con meeting

After months (or weeks) of planning, you'll finally get to meet the hotel staff you've been working with to produce your event. For very small meetings (such as a board meeting), the meeting may just be between you and your CSM. For large meetings (or meetings that represent high revenue generation for the hotel), every department manager will be in the room.

The meeting generally takes this format:

1. The CSM introduces the meeting planner.
2. The CSM asks each department manager to introduce himself.
3. The meeting planner talks about the meeting (its history and objectives), the attendees, and

any special information (for example, if this is your industry's most important event).

4. Depending on the complexity of the meeting, most department managers will excuse themselves so they can get back to work. The reservation, banquet, catering, and audiovisual directors, and their key staff, all stay at the meeting, as does the CSM.

5. The reservations manager will review your group's room reservations and give you the most up-to-date copy of your group's rooming list. You'll discuss your final pick up (and how many rooms are left, if any). You'll also review your VIP list for the front desk staff. The reservation director then leaves the meeting.

6. You'll review Banquet Event Orders (BEOs). You will walk through your entire meeting by reading each BEO. You'll review setups, explain flow of attendees from event to event, and consider potential problems. You'll also discuss any changes (a speaker decides he needs an overhead projector instead of a slide projector or you need to add a small meeting for one of your board committees, for example).

7. You'll review the venue's emergency/disaster procedures (medical emergencies, dangerous weather, fire, labor strikes). You are in charge of the meeting; your attendees will look to you in an emergency. You must be ready to take action—and you must know what action to take. You should make the procedures known—in writing—to key people on your staff, including the program chairman and everyone who will be manning the registration desk.

The pre-con is a rehearsal of your event. The process generally takes between a half hour to two or three hours. The pre-con will give you a nice comfort level when you see that the venue's staff has a good understanding of your event and they're all set to get to work for you.

Tips:

1. Ask for setup times. I always find out approximately when food functions will begin to be set or what time they'll begin setting up meeting rooms. That way, I know what time to walk through to check that everything is happening and can alert the hotel if I detect that something isn't getting done on time.

2. Get a listing of the department managers and their key staff along with their phone extensions. It's good to have everyone's name so you can contact them and also so that you have their full names when it is time to distribute gratuities.

To do

Once your pre-con ends, you turn to the following tasks.

1. Walk through the venue to familiarize yourself with the location of your meeting rooms, rest rooms, telephones, and restaurant outlets. (Also note if there are ATM machines or anything else that may be of interest to attendees.)

2. If you have an on-site office, have your boxes brought up to it. Unpack your boxes and organize your office space. Bring a laptop or rent a computer (and printer). You'll put them to good use making new name badges, printing out notices for attendees, making signs, and doing last minute work.

Keep the boxes for shipping back to the office after your meeting.

2. Put together registration packages.

3. Review the staff schedule and registration desk procedures.

4. Set a time to train the staff. You need to determine what will be said to each attendee as he comes to the desk and what material goes to him, where to direct attendees, and what to do if there is a problem. Even if it feels silly, have staff members practice saying their welcomes and handing the material to each other. This practice will make you all seem like naturals during the actual registration.

It's also a good idea to put instructions in writing. Figure 11.1 shows simple instructions for a banquet registration table staff. (Badges and badge holders were laid out on two six-foot tables. We stored office supplies (pens, on-site registration forms, and the like) under the table where they were hidden by table skirting.)

Figure 11.1

To:	Registration table staff
From:	Fern Dickey
Event:	Fellowship Society Dinner
Date:	Monday, October 26
Site:	Chicago Historical Society
Location:	First Floor Lobby
Time:	4:00 p.m.

Thanks so much for your help. The following needs to be done upon your arrival:

1. Set up registration desk, which will be at the front entrance of the society. (All other entrances will be locked, so attendees won't miss the registration table.)

- Pin event banner to front of table.
- Lay badges out on table in alphabetical order.
- Put name badge holders in bowls.

People will stop by the desk to pick up their name badge and materials. Let them select the type of badge holder they would like. Direct them to the cocktail hour, which is being held in the Portrait Gallery. (You will have maps at the desk.) Let them know that they can view the galleries during the cocktail hour.

After everything is set up, take a walk around and get oriented so that you will be able to direct guests to: telephones, bathrooms, elevator, coat check, etc. Be ready for the first guests to arrive between 4:45 and 5:00 p.m.

2. Photography Session: Fellowship inductees will arrive early for a 5:30 p.m. photography session. (List of inductees attached.) They should be directed to the spiral staircase on the second floor.

3. Potential problems:

- Name misspelled on badge. There are extra name badges so you can hand write a new one if necessary. (Keep the wrong one and note the correct spelling so we can change the database when we get back to the office)
- No name badge. Hand write a name badge. (Take a business card or get the person's name, as we need this info for registration/billing.)
- The person wants to change his meal ticket for another selection. Take back the meal ticket, issue a new one, and keep a checklist of all changes so we can alert the catering company.

(If anyone asks, there are no reserved tables except for the guest of honor.)

4. We ask that while you are at the registration desk you please:
  - Refrain from chewing gum, eating, or leaving drinks on the registration table.
  - Try to keep the table organized as people take their badges. It may get a little crazy, as people tend to come in waves.

· Man the desk until 6:45 p.m., and then pack up leftover materials and put them in the coat check.

Thank you again for your assistance,
Fern

Tip: For conferences, put together a daily schedule for your on-site staff. This way everyone is clear about their hours, responsibilities, and break times. This will also help everyone know where everyone else can be found at any given time.

Opening day

It's hard to sleep the night before the big event. A million questions run through your mind: Will there be enough food? Will my temporary help show up? Will the keynote speaker be any good? Will everything flow as I planned? This is natural!

In the morning, begin setting up early. If the registration desk opens to the public at 8 a.m., be downstairs by 6 a.m. You'll need to get the registration area set up and ready to go before your attendees show up, and you don't want to be seen rushing around.

Tip: Never hand out registration material before your registration posted times. It happens when your early birds are downstairs milling around your registration desk with coffee and the paper. Naturally, they'd like to pick up their registration material while you're setting up. Politely tell them the registration desk officially opens at [TIME]. Otherwise you'll have people lining up before you're officially open. If you're busy handing out packets, you won't have your registration desk set up on time, and you'll look unprofessional.

Registration desk and meeting room setups

If the room or table is available, do as much as you can the day before. On the front table or counter we usually put the registration envelopes in two boxes: an A–M box and an N–Z box, so that attendees can form two lines. (You may want to break it down even further if you've got the staff.) Extra daily schedules can be on the front desk too. Keep it neat and organized. Stack bulky handout materials, canvas bags, and spouse/guest bags on back tables.

Once registration is set, you're off to check your meeting rooms.

1. Pre-session:
- Put out session signs.
- Make sure each table has full pitchers of water, glasses, notepads, and pencils.
- Check the number of chairs.
- Check the audiovisual setup against your Banquet Event Orders (Tip: Always check to make sure the flip chart markers aren't dry.)
- Put out handouts and evaluation forms.
- Make sure your door monitors — if you have or need them — are set to collect tickets or monitor sign-in sheets
- Check hotel reader boards to make sure they're listing the correct rooms and times.

2. During sessions (look in several times):
- Check for sound bleed from other rooms
- See if the speaker needs assistance
- Check the general tone of the room and to make sure everyone is comfortable.

3. Post-session:
- Walk through the meeting room and collect evaluation forms that were left on the tables.

☺ Take your signs. (Anything you leave will be tossed out.)

☺ Make sure rooms are being refreshed if there are other sessions following.

Now take a deep breath. The program has started and it will take on a life of its own. You're just going to be checking to make sure everything is happening as planned and on schedule, and you'll solve problems as they crop up. And they will. The good news is, everything has a solution. The relationship you've built with your CSM will hold you in good stead because he'll be your guardian angel when it comes to keeping the event flowing smoothly and solving the crises that will pop up.

You

Even though you're "just" the meeting planner and your organization's executives are on site as well, you are the person the attendees will look to—for the mood of the event, for help in an emergency, for problem-solving. They know you. Many of them will have spoken with you over the phone before the meeting, and you'll talk with many of them on site. If you have a good attitude—you're smiling, calm, and in control—you will make everyone else feel comfortable. The old adage is true: Never let them see you sweat.

Daily banquet event order checks

At the end of each day, the CSM or the catering director will bring you your daily bills to review. They'll include everything you've ordered for that day. Don't just sign the bills. Tell the CSM that you'll review them overnight and return them first thing in the morning. This will give you a chance to carefully check them against your BEOs.

Crises

A crisis does not have to mean a fire or a medical emergency. During one of our conferences, a seven-piece band began rehearsing for a wedding in the room next to my general session. The sound was bleeding through the wall — loudly. I found my CSM and we came up with a compromise. The band held off its rehearsal for 20 minutes and we moved our group into another room when it became available.

However, be prepared for real crises. Know procedures and share them with others via announcements, which should be typed and available to the session moderator, your staff, and other session officials.

Meeting wrap-up

Once your attendees have left the final session, you have two things to do. First, pack up any material to be shipped back to the office. (There will be noticeably fewer boxes to pack.) Second, distribute gratuities to the people who've helped make your meeting a success.

Shipping back to the office

Pack up and label your boxes. (Remember to bring your own packing tape and labels so that you don't have to buy them from the hotel.) Contact the venue's shipping department. You'll fill out a form and they'll take your boxes. It's that easy.

Gratuities and thank you notes

Write a thank-you note and enclose it in an envelope along with a gratuity to thank the hotel staff who've worked hard on your behalf. As amazing as it is, the meetings industry has not established standards for tipping. It's a gray area, but there are suggested formulas for how much to tip and to whom. Here are some of them:

- The budget for gratuities is based on a percentage of the total hotel bill. (I've done this and usually budget for 2 to 4 percent of the total hotel expenses. I've read this can range all the way to 15 percent, which seems very high.)

- Budget a set amount per attendee (between $1 and $5). If you have 400 attendees and you decide you're going to budget to tip based on $5 per attendee, your tipping budget is $2,000.

- Meeting Professionals International (*www.mpiweb.org*; (972) 702-3000) publishes an "All-Purpose Tipping Guide," ($5 for members; $7 for nonmembers) that provides a "quick reference on who, why and when to tip, including acceptable, cost-saving nonmonetary gifts. Confidently tip everyone, from the bellman to the catering director and the convention service team." Its guidelines vary from percentage tips for bartenders and wine stewards to specific amounts for the CMS and bell staff. Because tipping has no standard, I'd advise purchasing this and using it as a guideline.

Tips:

- Keep a running list of people who've helped you during the event. If a shipping staffer has been extra good to me by helping me open and unpack boxes, I make sure I write his name down on my list so that I remember to tip him.

- There are lots of behind-the-scenes people who you'll never meet or talk to, such as the housekeeping manager, the switchboard manager, and the shipping/receiving manager. Ask your CSM to tell you who they are so that you may tip them.

☉ Left over items, such as extra canvas bags or t-shirts, make nice gifts to people in the hotel who may not normally receive tips. Talk to your CSM about distribution.

Post-meeting

Often, after large or important meetings, your staff and your advisory committee (if you have one) will meet on site for 15 or 20 minutes. You'll discuss comments you've heard from attendees, talk about your general reactions, and list the things that went well and the things you'd change for future events. Take notes. This information will be valuable as you plan future events.

This meeting should be planned well in advance. Reserve a room for this meeting during your planning process.

Back at the office

Post-meeting activities are important, but most of them are not deemed "necessary" — after all, your meeting is over — and are often put on the backburner. Do them. *They're important.* They generate goodwill, help maintain your reputation as a first-class planner, and keep you in good stead when you plan future events. Here's a list of what we do when we're back at the office:

☉ Send thank you letters to attendees, speakers, hotel staff, and vendors.

☉ Upon receipt, review invoices and submit bills to accounting for payment.

- ⏲ Write a post-meeting wrap-up report.
- ⏲ Tabulate final evaluations into summary report.
- ⏲ Prepare a demographic report for marketing purposes. (This will help you understand the profile of the typical attendee so that you can buy lists that match those criteria. Examples include job titles, sales volume of company, location, and primary product or service sold.)
- ⏲ Prepare and maintain hotel history reports, including costs and number of sleeping rooms.
- ⏲ Unpack boxes.
- ⏲ Collect any money due/issue refunds.

Conclusion

Quick steps

1. Elect someone to man the home base.
2. Make sure boxes have arrived at the venue.
3. Attend the pre-con.
4. Set up your registration desk.
5. Do daily walk-throughs to check meeting room setups.

Quick tips

- ⏲ Work with your CSM to ensure the meeting flows smoothly
- ⏲ Be prepared for anything to happen — and maintain your cool when it does.

Appendix

Alternate meeting methods (teleconferencing, audio conferencing, video conferencing, webcasting)

AT&T
www.att.com
(800) 232-1234
Offers audio and video conferencing, as well as various Internet services.

Conference America
www.yourcall.com
(800) 925-8000
Offers teleconferencing and webcasting services.

WebCasting, Inc.
www.webcasting.com
(972) 432-8700
A full-service broadcast and multimedia development company specializing in audio/video production, streaming, and webcasting.

Books

The Convention Liaison Council Manual, 6th edition. Edited by Lincoln H. Colby, CMP. The Convention Liaison Council, Washington, DC: 1994.

Gale's Encyclopedia of Associations (updated annually). Gale Research Inc. (800) 877-4253
Your local library will have this book in its reference room.

Planning Successful Meetings and Events.
Ann. J. Boehme.
AMACOM, New York: 1999.

Professional Meeting Management, 3rd edition.
Edited by Edward G. Polivka.
Professional Convention Management Association, Birmingham, AL: 1996.

Corporate Training Facilities

AT&T Learning Center
300 North Maple Avenue
Basking Ridge, NJ 07920
(908) 953-3000.

Xerox Document University
Training and Conference
Center
Rts. 7 & 659
Leesburg, VA 20176
United States
www.xeroxdocu.com
(703) 724-6152
(703) 729-5382 fax

Knowledge Development
Centers
www.kdc.inc.com
*18 centers throughout the U.S.
with plans for more. Offers training suites and development labs
that include the latest in high-tech
equipment, communications, and
comfort, as well as technical and
management support and superior
customer services.*

Legal Advice

Jonathan Howe
Howe & Hutton, Ltd.
20 North Wacker Drive
Chicago, IL 60606
(312) 263-3001
(312) 372-6685 fax
E-mail: jth@howehutton.com

John S. Foster, III
Attorney at Law
Suite 1009
1447 Peachtree Street, NE
Atlanta, GA 30309
(404) 873-5200
(404) 873-6560 fax
E-mail:
jsfoster@mindspring.com

Meeting Industry Magazines and Directories

Association Meetings
Adams Business Media/
Meetings Group
43L Nason Street
Maynard, MA 01754
www.meetingsnet.com
(978) 897-5552

Convene
www.pcma.org
*A publication of the Professional
Convention Management Association.*

*The Guide to Unique Meeting
Facilities*
Amarc, Inc.
P.O. Box 279
Minturn, CO 81645
www.theguide.com
(970) 827-5500
(970) 827-9411 fax

Meeting News
One Penn Plaza
New York, NY 10119
www.meetingnews.com
Contact: Elaine Cipriano,
Managing Editor

The Meeting Professional
www.mpiweb.org
A publication of Meeting Professionals International.

Meetings & Conventions
500 Plaza Drive
Secaucus, NJ 07094
Contact: Lori Cioffi, Editor in Chief
www.meetings-conventions.com
(201) 902-1786
(201) 319-1976 fax

Successful Meetings
770 Broadway
New York, NY 10003
www.successmtgs.com
(646) 654-5049
(646) 654-7265 fax

Meeting Industry and Related Associations

American Society of Association Executives
1575 I St., N.W.
Washington, DC 20005-1103
www.asaenet.org
(202) 626-2723
(202) 626-2803 TDD
(202) 371-8825 fax

Association of Destination Management Executives
3333 Quebec Street
Suite 4050
Denver, CO 80207
www.adme.org

(303) 394-3905
(303) 394-3450 fax

International Association of Convention & Visitor Bureaus
2000 L Street, NW
Suite 702
Washington, DC 20036
www.iacvb.org
(202) 296-7888
(202) 296-7889 fax

International Association For Exposition Management
P.O. Box 802425
Dallas, TX 75380
(972) 458-8119
(972) 458-8119 fax

International Congress & Convention Association
North America Regional Office:
8414 Westmont Terrace
Bethesda, MD 20817
www.icca.nl
(301) 365 5238
(301) 365 8026 fax

International Association of Conference Centers
IACC North America
243 North Lindbergh Boulevard
St. Louis, MO 63141
www.iacconline.com
(314) 993-8575
(314) 993-8919 fax

Meeting Professionals International International Headquarters
4455 LBJ Freeway
Suite 1200

Dallas, TX 75244-5903
www.mpiweb.org
(972) 702-3000
(972) 702-3070 fax

The Professional Convention
Management Association
100 Vestavia Parkway
Suite 220
Birmingham, AL 35216-3743
www.pcma.org
(205) 823-7262
(205) 822-3891 fax
(877) 827-7262 customer service
hotline
(877) 495-7262 fax-on-demand
service

Online Sources

AgendaOnline
www.agendaonline.com
*A business-to-business directory
providing relevant information
about services that event planners
need to plan and produce special
events.*

AllMeetings
www.allmeetings.com
*An award-winning search engine
that compares your meeting cost
(including airfare) at thousands of
hotels.*

American Society of Composers, Authors and Publishers
www.ascap.com
For music licensing.

American Society of Media
Photographers
www.asmp.org
Search for local photographers.

Broadcast Music, Inc. (BMI)
www.bmi.com
For music licensing.

B-there.com
www.b-there.com
*Offers an attendee "relationship
management" service.*

Conferon (Corporate Office)
www.conferon.com
*The largest independent meeting-
planning firm in the United
States.*

Event411.com, Inc.
www.event411.com
*One of the first and one of the
largest online event planning
firms.*

EventSource.com, Inc.
www.eventsource.com
*The Internet's first and largest
e-commerce business-to-business
service for meeting planners
worldwide.*

HotDatesHotRates
www.hdhr.com
*Facilities post open space here that
they can't fill and will offer it at a
reduced (hot) rate.*

The Innkeeper's Register
www.innbook.com
Contains a database of 365 of the best country inns and bed & breakfasts in the United States and Canada.

Meeting In-Site Corp.
www.meetingin-site.com
E-mail: meetings@meetingin-site.com
Offers meeting planning services, but can also help you find temporary help in the meeting planning field.

Meetings Industry Mall
www.mim.com
Contact: Rodman J. Marymor, CMP, Managing Partner
Find information on locations, services, products, venues, travel, and "cool tools" (such as currency, weather, and traffic).

MeetingPlannerTips.com
www.meetingplannertips.com
MeetingsNet
www. meetingsnet.com
Offers a multitude of online resources, such as timelines, tips, checklists, guides, and links to other online resources.

Momentix
www.momentix.com
Online registration management.

Passkey.com, Inc.
www.passkey.com
Offers housing, registration, and travel services.

PlanSoft
www.plansoft.com
The leading provider of meeting technology tools.

Primeshot.com
www.primeshot.com
Book photographers, and also give your attendees on-site access to view and share event photos in password-protected galleries.

SeeUthere.com
www.seeUthere.com
A partner of PlanSoft. Offers registration services and has been getting rave reviews.

Promotion Resources

American Institute of Graphic Artists
164 Fifth Avenue
New York, NY 10010
www.aiga.org
(212) 807-1990
Search for a designer.

Robert Bly
22 East Quackenbush Avenue, 3rd Floor
Dumont, NJ 07628
www.bly.com
(201) 385-1220
(201) 385-1138 fax
An independent copywriter and consultant with 20 years of

experience in business-to-business, high-tech, industrial, and direct marketing. Full of how-to articles (including the latest on e-marketing) and vendor resources.

Copywriter's Council of America
P.O. Box 102
Middle Island, NY
(631) 924-8555
(631) 924-3890 fax
A reference to find copywriters.

Council of Public Relations Firms
11 Penn Plaza, Fifth Floor
New York, NY 10001
www.prfirms.org
(877) 773-4767
(877) PRFAXES

Ralph D. Elliott, Ph.D.
Director of Professional Development
Clemson University
Clemson, SC 29634
(864) 656-3983
(864) 656-0900 fax
E-mail: elliot@clemson.edu
A seminar/conference marketing teacher offering seminars and books.

The Direct Marketing Association
1120 Avenue of the Americas
New York, NY 10036-6700
www.the-dma.org
(212) 768-7277

(212) 302-6714 fax
The oldest and largest trade association for users and suppliers in the direct, database, and interactive marketing fields.

The Graphic Arts Information Network (GAIN)
www.gain.com
The site's online service, PrintAccess, an electronic buyers' guide for the printing and graphic communications industry, showcases PIA member companies, including:

Printing Industries of America
100 Daingerfield Road
Alexandria, VA 22314
(703) 519-8100
(703) 545-3227 fax

and

Graphic Arts Technical Foundation
200 Deer Run Road
Sewickley, PA 15143
(412) 741-6860
(412) 741-2311 fax

Graphic Artists Guild
90 John Street
Suite 403
New York, NY 10038-3202
www.gag.org
(800) 500-2672
(212) 791-0333
Search for graphic artists in fields ranging from illustration to Web

design. You can review portfolios online.

Jackie Pantaliano, CME
President
ImPRessions Public Relations and Publicity
12 Orleans Road
Parsippany, NJ 07054-4032
(973) 884-4740
(973) 884-3122 fax
E-mail: Pantaliano@aol.com

Alice Meliere
KDS Group
135 Kinnelon Road
Suite 104
Kinnelon, NJ 07405
(973) 492-5652
(973) 283-4380 fax
E-mail: kdsgroup@aol.com
Design, promotion, and marketing.

National Association for Printing Leadership (NAPL)
75 West Century Road
Paramus, New Jersey 07652
www.napl.org
(201) 634-9600 or (800)642-6275
A printing industry trade organization that can give you a list of printers either in a specific geographic area or printing specialty.

Public Relations Society of America
33 Irving Place
New York, NY 10003-2376

www.prsa.org
(212) 995-2230
Search for a PR firm.

Edith Roman Associates, Inc.
Blue Hill Plaza, 16th Floor
P.O. Box 1556
Pearl River, NY 10965-3104
www.edithroman.com
(914) 620-9000 or (800) 223-2194
(914) 620-9035 fax
Resource-rich Web site on direct marketing.

Smartsource Corporation
200 Wheeler Road
Burlington, MA 01803
www.smartsourceonline.com
(800) 239-0239
(781) 229-7673 fax
An outsource for doing e-mail and fax broadcasts.

Catherine Vitale
M2 Design
370 Knickerbocker Road
Englewood, NJ 07632
(201) 569-9559
(201) 569-1226 fax
E-mail: woofiesmom@aol.com
Graphic design services.

Speaker Associations and Bureaus

Greater Talent Network, Inc
150 Fifth Avenue, Suite 900
New York, NY 10011
www.greatertalent.com

(212) 645-4200 or (800) 326-4211
(212) 627-1471 fax

International Speakers Bureau
2528 Elm Street
Suite 200
Dallas, TX 75226
www.isbspeakers.com
(214) 744-3885 or (800) 842-4483
(214) 744-3888 fax

Leading Authorities, Inc.
919 18th Street, NW
Suite 500
Washington, DC 20006
www.leadingauthorities.com
(800) SPEAKER

Leigh Bureau
1065 US Hwy 22
Third Floor
Bridgewater, NJ 08807
www.leighbureau.com
(908) 253-8600
(908) 253-8601 fax

National Speakers Association
1500 South Priest Drive
Tempe, AZ 85281
www.nsaspeaker.org
(480) 968-2552
(480) 968-0911 fax

Web sites to find Meeting-Related Vendors, Suppliers, and Services

American Society of Association Executives (ASAE)
www.asaenet.org

Click on "Find Associations, People, Business," and go to the buyer's guide on the click-down menu.

Corbin Ball
Corbin Ball Associates
506 14th Street
Bellingham, WA 98225
www.corbinball.com
(360) 734-8756
(508) 632-7730 fax
Email: corbin@corbinball.com
The "tips & tools" section seems to have it all and claims to be the meeting industry's most comprehensive listing of categorized Web sites.

Eventsource
www.eventsource.com
Click on "Resource Center" for listings of vendors and suppliers.

Meeting Industry Mall
www.mim.com

Successful Meetings Magazine
www.successmtgs.com
Click on "Help for Meeting Planners" and then go to the "Web Site Directory."

Glossary of Meeting Terms

Acceptance — signature on a contract.

Acknowledgment — the written notice sent to a guest that his or her room reservation request has been received and is being processed.

Act of God clause — the part of a contract that releases both parties from liability in the event that something happens that is out of their control (hurricane, tornado, war, etc.).

Actual budget — the current budget that exists in fact or reality.

Advance deposit — the amount of money paid to secure a room, facility, or service in advance.

Advance registration — a registration policy that allows attendees to register for a event before it actually takes place; done through mail, phone, Internet or fax.

Advertising — the information about a meeting that the organization pays to have printed or announced in various forms of media.

Agenda — a list, outline, or plan of items to be done or considered at a meeting or during a specific time block.

Amenities — things that are conducive to material comfort or convenience.

American Society of Composers and Publishers (ASCAP) — a major U.S. music licensing organization.

Americans with Disabilities Act (ADA) — a civil rights statute passed in 1990 to meet the needs of disabled people.

Ancillary activities — all meeting support services within a facility that generate revenue.

Arbitration—a procedure devised to resolve a dispute outside of the court system.

Arrival pattern—specific days and time blocks when attendees are expected to arrive.

Attendee data—demographic information about each attendee.

Attrition—the reduction of the room block reserved for a meeting.

Audio conferencing—live conference communication using telephone lines; an audio signal can be played into a meeting room.

Authorized signature—the signature of a person with the legal power and influence to make a decision; a requirement of all valid contracts.

Auxiliary business—business that is brought to the facility because of, or in conjunction with, a meeting.

Auxiliary services—contracted services that provide meeting support.

Backup material—the actual receipts and other documents concerning charges made to the master account; this should accompany the final invoice.

Badge—an adhesive, pin, or clip-on tag with identifying information that is given to each registrant.

Balance sheet—a statement of financial status at a given time (liabilities, assets, etc.).

Banquet—an elaborate, and often ceremonious, meal for numerous people, often in honor of a particular person.

Banquet Event Order (BEO)—a facility form that provides details to staff concerning the meeting manager's requirements for room setup, food and beverage, etc.

Bid—a statement of what one will give or take in return for something else (a price); a proposal.

Blanket license—permission granted by a performing rights society to play any music in its repertoire.

Board of directors style—a long double-width table arrangement for conferences.

Book—to reserve in advance; to enter, write, or register so as to engage transportation or reserve lodging.

Booking policy—guidelines by which a convention center prioritizes reservations; this may correspond to hotel rooms the event will use in the area.

Breakout session—small discussion groups that work together on a specific task after the whole group has received similar instruction or information.

Broadcast fax — a service which transmits a fax to a large number of people.

Broadcast Music, Inc. (BMI) — a major U.S. music licensing organization.

Business casual — a style of dress that is less formal than a standard office suit and tie or dress and heels.

Business center services — services that allow attendees to keep in touch with their offices (phone, fax, messages, etc.).

Bus staff — personnel who remove dirty dishes and reset tables in a restaurant or hotel.

Call brand — a medium-priced brand of alcohol.

Cancellation clause — a contract item that specifies damages that apply if either party terminates the agreement.

Cancellation insurance — a policy secured by a facility or organization to provide compensation for income lost due to an event's cancellation.

Cancellation policy — a written statement of actions that can or will be taken in the event of a cancellation due to a specific circumstance.

Cash bar — a type if bar service in which attendees pay for their own drinks.

Catering manager — person in the facility who is responsible for catering events.

Chamber of commerce — an association of businesspeople who promote commercial and industrial interests in a community.

Charter — to hire, rent, or lease for exclusive and temporary use.

Chef's table — an opportunity for the meeting manager to sample a menu in advance of the event.

City-wide meeting — a meeting that requires the use of a convention center and multiple hotels in the host city.

Classroom style — a seating arrangement in which rows of tables face the presenter and each person has a space for writing.

Clause — a detailed section of a contract pertaining to a specific issue.

Common carrier — a company that transports people, goods, or messages for a fee.

Complete meeting package — an all-inclusive plan offered at conference centers that includes meals, lodging, and support services.

Complimentary room — space given at no charge.

Concierge — a hotel staff member who handles luggage and mail, makes reservations, and arranges other matters for guests.

Concurrent sessions — sessions occurring at the same time.

Conference center — a facility that is constructed for and devoted to meetings (more meeting space than sleeping rooms).

Conference style — a seating arrangement where chairs are placed around all sides of a table.

Confirmation — verification of the existence of a reservation; an informal letter outlining the preliminary plans for the use of a facility or service (for small suppliers, this may serve as a contract).

Confirmation letter — a letter to speakers acknowledging that a commitment has been made by the speaker and the organization and outlining information about the meeting.

Confirmed reservation — an oral or written agreement by a facility to accept a request for an accommodation that must state the intent of the parties, the particular date, the rate, type of accommodations and the number to be accommodated (without this information, the agreement is not binding); oral agreements may require guest credit card number.

Conflict of interest statement — a written document requiring speakers to disclose any conflicts of interest that may be created by their involvement with another organization.

Continuing education units — a requirement of many professional groups by which members must certify participation in formal educational programs designed to maintain their level of ability beyond their original certification date.

Contract — an agreement, with legally sufficient consideration, between competent parties to provide a particular service, the breach of which involves a legal penalty.

Contracted service — a service for which the meeting manager bargains or negotiates a formal contract.

Contractor — a party who legally agrees, in writing, to perform work or provide a service.

Convention services manager (CSM) — a person who assists the meeting manager in arranging details of a meeting and coordinating the efforts of various service suppliers at the meeting site

Convention and visitors bureau (CVB) — a nonprofit marketing organization representing a community in the solicitation and servicing of all types of visitors to that destination.

Copyright — the exclusive legal right to reproduce, publish, or sell literary, musical, or artistic work.

Copyright waiver — the written authorization from a speaker that an organization may record their presentation for sale or future use.

Demographic profile — a summary of the statistical characteristics of attendees (age, income, etc.).

Demographics — statistical characteristics, such as age, occupation, income level, etc.

Destination management company (DMC) — local supplier who can arrange, manage, and/or plan any function or service for a meeting.

Destination marketing — publicity targeted at promoting a particular location as a meeting site and/or tourist attraction.

Direct mail — a marketing technique in which information is mailed (or e-mailed) directly to individuals in the target audience.

Double booking — the occurrence of two or more groups or individuals being promised the same space over the same time frame.

Double room — a room for two people with one bed (double, queen, or king).

Dram shop laws — laws designed to protect individuals who are injured due to the negligence of a person intoxicated by drugs or alcohol.

Dress code — a generally accepted means of attire.

Duoserve property — a hotel property in which logistics are handled by the CSM, with catering handled by a separate manager.

Duty roster — a list outlining the hourly schedules and responsibilities of all meeting staff members.

Emergency medical plan — a formalized plan of action for handling on-site emergencies from basic first aid to fire or serious injury.

Evaluation — the process of gathering specific information related to goals and objectives.

Event order (EO) — see Function sheet.

Exclusive contract — a contract between a facility and a service as the only service that may be used in that facility for a specific service.

Exhibit — an organization's booth at a public show for competition, demonstration, or sale.

Expense budget — a detailed list of expense items for a meeting and the funds allocated or estimated for each.

Facilitator — the person assigned to make a meeting or discussion run smoothly and efficiently.

Facility specification format — a standard form, or form used by a specific facility, to record details of a meeting.

Final statement — the master billing account in its final form, after the event is over.

Fixed expense — a budget item that is constant (that is, not dependent on attendance).

Flat room rate—a basic rate with no discount or special offer.

Floor plan—a scaled drawing showing the arrangement of rooms, halls, and so on.

Function—an event that is a part of a planned meeting; an area of meeting planning that involves income or expenses (printing, registration, etc.).

Function room—a room in which a formal event is held.

Function sheet—a collection of all details relative to a meeting's needs (including sleeping rooms, billing arrangements, contractor information, etc.); this document is circulated to all key personnel in the facility and organization.

Function space—the physical space taken up by an event.

Function ticket—a ticket for admission to an event that is part of the planned meeting activities.

General session—a session that all participants in a meeting attend.

Goods and services tax—a fee imposed on the sale of goods and services.

Gratuity—cash or a gift amounting to a percentage of the bill that is given to managers and department heads after an event for exceptional service provided.

Group history—facts and figures detailing a group's past events.

Group rate—a room rate negotiated for booking multiple guests, usually reflecting a percentage reduction from the rack rate.

Head count—the number of people physically present at an event.

Headquarters hotel—one hotel in a multiple hotel meeting where VIPs stay and official functions are held.

Hold all space—a blanket hold on all available space in a facility without specific meeting or function room names.

Hold harmless clause—a part of a contract declaring that neither party will hold the other responsible for any damages or theft to materials or equipment owned or rented by either party; a clause declaring that one party will take responsibility for damages assessed as the result of another party's inaction.

Hospitality suite/room—a suite or room arranged for the convenience, comfort, and socialization of guests, often with drinks and snacks available.

Host—the person assigned to assist a speaker before, during, and after a presentation.

Hosted bar—a type of bar service in which the sponsor pays for all drinks.

Housing bureau—third party agency capable of managing the housing process for a meeting.

Housing list — a list of all guests provided by the meeting manager detailing room requirements, special guests, payment method, etc.

Housing report — a document prepared by a housing bureau detailing the housing process (reservations, pick up, etc.).

Housing service — a service that handles booking rooms for meetings using multiple hotel facilities.

Incidentals — minor expense items that are not usually itemized.

Income budget — a detailed list of income sources for a meeting and the funds expected from each.

In conjunction with (ICW) — an event or function that occurs because of another meeting.

Indemnified — secured against loss or hurt; held harmless.

Insurance — a legal agreement by which one party guarantees to undertake loss suffered by the other under specific circumstances.

International association of convention and visitors bureaus (IACVB) — a worldwide authority on destination marketing dedicated to the promotion of professional practices in the solicitation and servicing of meetings and conventions.

International association of conference centers (IACC) — a worldwide authority on the convention center which sets standards for membership including such areas as conference center design, operation, and service.

Inventory list — a detailed, itemized list of supplies and equipment on hand.

Invitation letter — a letter to a potential speaker outlining the preliminary purpose and plans of a meeting and requesting his or her services.

Invoice — an itemized list, with prices, of goods or services sold or shipped.

Itinerary — the actual or proposed route and schedule of travel.

Keynote — a meeting's opening remarks, which set the tone of the event and motivate attendees.

Keynote speaker — one who presents the issues of primary interest to a group of people.

Labor union — a workforce organization requiring various rules to be followed by the employing facility advocating the well-being of workers.

Lavaliere microphone — a small microphone that is clipped onto clothing to allow the speaker to move around while speaking.

Lectern — an elevated stand for reading materials to be used during a presentation.

Lectern microphone — a microphone attached directly to a lectern on a flexible metal goose neck.

Legal authority — the position of a person within an organization or facility that enables them to sign an agreement on behalf of the organization or facility.

Letter of agreement — a letter from the facility being considered indicating the space requested and held; followed by negotiations.

Liability — something that an organization is legally responsible for.

Liability clause — a part of a contract outlining conditions of liability.

Liability disclaimer — a legal statement releasing the organization from responsibility for any arrangements made by attendees with services listed by the organization (i.e., childcare).

Liability law — a system of laws designed to protect people from damages caused by a party behaving in a negligent manner and creating or being responsible for harm as the result of that behavior.

License — written permission granted by an authority to engage in a specific action or business.

Limited consumption bar — a type of bar service in which the host establishes the maximum dollar amount to be spent at an open bar, and when that limit is reached, the bar is closed or converted to cash bar.

Liquidated damage clause — contract language that specifies the exact amount of money parties agree to pay for breach of the contract.

Liquidated damages — the amount of money one party must pay to the other in the event of a breach of contract.

Mailing house — a company equipped to handle bulk mailings on behalf of an organization.

Mailing list — a list of names to whom literature or information is sent.

Maitre d' — the head waiter at a hotel or restaurant.

Marketing — the process of selling a meeting to the target audience.

Master billing account — a centralized record of all charges associated with a meeting.

Media kit — a packet of information that is supplied to the media containing all the details of a meeting that are required to attract media attention and attendees.

Meet and greet — an escort service provided to VIP guests at the airport.

Meeting history — facts and details concerning previous meetings.

Meeting profile — a written report outlining statistics of previous meetings, the anticipated use of all services, a profile of attendees, an occupancy pattern, etc.

Meeting resume — see Function sheet.

Moderator — one who presides over an assembly, meeting, or discussion.

Needs analysis — an organized and planned process of identifying needs.

Networking — the exchange of information or services among individuals, groups, or institutions.

News (press) release — an official statement about a meeting that is sent to the media for printing in various publications.

No-show report — a report that states the percent of attendees who fail to show up but who did not cancel their reservations.

Objectives — formalized statements of outcomes to be anticipated as a result of the educational process.

Occupancy rate — number of single vs. double occupancy rooms used by attendees.

Official airline — an airline contracted by the sponsor of an event to provide special deals or amenities to attendees.

Off-site event — an event held somewhere other than the host facility.

On-site office — an organization's temporary headquarters office that is set up on site to handle business during the event.

On-site registration — registration that occurs directly before the meeting at the meeting location.

Open bar — a type of bar service in which drinks are paid for by the sponsoring organization.

Outside vendor — suppliers who are not directly associated with the facility.

Outsourcing — obtaining the services of a third party contractor to handle some aspect of the meeting.

Overbooking — a practice by which a hotel books the same accommodations twice in anticipation of a certain cancellation rate, based on past no-show rates.

Paid-out slips — a method of paying tips and gratuities by which an employee is given a slip to present to the facility cashier for payment; the amount is added to the meeting's master account.

Paper trail — written records of all business dealings that can be reviewed if questions arise (documentation).

Peak hotel room night pick up — the number of hotel room nights used on the busiest night of an event.

Pick up — the number of rooms actually used each day of an event.

Pick-up report — a post-meeting document detailing the number of rooms used each day of an event.

Planner's professional liability — a type of insurance for the meeting manager that covers damages claimed due to negligence.

Planning matrix — a grid used to plan meeting formats and finalize subject areas, topics, and assignments.

Plenary sessions — general assemblies for all participants.

Podium — a small raised platform for a presenter to stand on.

Post-conference meeting (post-con) — a meeting between a meeting manager and staff to discuss and evaluate the event as soon as it is over.

Pre- and post-meeting tours — recreational tours scheduled right before or after the meeting to encourage socialization among attendees.

Pre-conference meeting (pre-con) — a meeting between the meeting manager, facility department heads, and major contractors prior to the start of the meeting.

Premium brand — the most expensive, high-quality brand of alcohol.

Presenter — a person who delivers a speech or program.

Press release — material sent to a newspaper before a prearranged date of publication to publicize a meeting.

Profile of attendees — data concerning attendees, including their average age, spending habits, etc.; also called the profile of meeting participants.

Program development — planning that takes place before a meeting regarding its specific content and format.

Projected budget — an outline of expected income and expenses.

Promotion — the aspect of marketing that deals with generating program awareness amongst the target audience.

Proposal — an offer or bid for goods or services.

Public relations — those functions of an organization concerned with informing the public and creating a favorable impression.

Publicity — free news items and editorials placed in third-party publications to generate interest in a meeting.

Rack rate — the price the public would generally pay for a sleeping room.

Reasonable accommodation — any provision that aids the participation of a person with a disability, as long as it does not create a hazard to others, a major disruption in business, or an undue financial or administrative burden.

Reception — a social gathering before an event.

Refund policy — an official, stated policy by which registration fees will be refunded.

Registrant — a person attending a meeting who is officially registered.

Registration — the process of signing up to attend a meeting or event.

Registration card/form — the card or form on which registrants record basic personal information, such as fee category (guest or attendee, early bird versus regular rate, etc.), breakout session selection, and contact info, and then forward it to the appropriate organization.

Registration data — information about an attendee that is gathered as part of the registration process (occupation, fee category, etc.).

Registration packet — information concerning the program and local attractions and services given to each registrant.

Reimbursement policy — a statement of procedures that speakers and personnel must follow in order to have their expenses reimbursed.

Report — a summary of statistical information and an analysis of what it indicates about the meeting.

Reservation request — a communication by which guests indicate sleeping room requirements; these are forwarded to the hotel to secure a reservation.

Resource manual — a packet of handouts from all sessions that will occur during the meeting.

Resume — see Function sheet.

Room block — the total number of sleeping rooms reserved.

Room capacity — the number of people that can function safely and comfortably in a room.

Room commitment — the rooms to be held open each night of the meeting, specified by room type (double, single, etc.).

Room deposit — the amount of money that must be paid for the hotel to guarantee to hold a room.

Room nights — the number of rooms times the number of nights each is used each day of the meeting

Room occupancy pattern — the number of single and double rooms used.

Room rate — the cost of a hotel room.

Schedule — a printed table of time and location of transportation service.

Security — uniformed professionals employed to ensure the safety of attendees, to protect the property of exhibitors, and to make certain that people not registered as attendees do not gain entrance.

Service charge — an amount automatically added to the room rate as a gratuity.

Shipping agent — a third-party company that handles shipping goods to and from a meeting.

Shuttle buses — buses contracted to transport attendees between various meeting facilities.

Signage — all informational and directional signs required for an event.

Single room — a room for one person with one bed (single, queen, or king).

Site inspection — the process by which the details of a potential location are evaluated.

Site selection — the process by which a location for the event is chosen.

Six-by-six rule — audiovisual guidelines by which no transparency or slide should contain more than six words per line of text and no more than six lines of text.

Skirting — an attractive fabric placed around a table to conceal the area underneath.

Slippage — a reduction in the number of rooms used from the original reserved block.

Speaker bureau — a broker or agent for many professional speakers.

Speaker preparation room — a room designated for speakers to use to prepare audiovisual materials, practice their speeches, etc.

Special block — a small block within the meeting's room block reserved for dignitaries or people with special needs.

Staging guide — a compilation of all function sheets, room setups, and other materials relevant to running the event.

Tabletop display — an exhibit in which materials are arranged on a tabletop (no booth).

Teleconferencing — technology that permits individuals to participate in regional, national, or worldwide meetings without actually leaving their local area; the live transmission of video or audio signals.

Temporary meeting personnel — temporary employees from the destination who are hired to perform various tasks at the event.

Termination clause — a part of a contract dealing with procedures, damages, and rights for terminating the agreement.

Theater style (auditorium style) — a seating arrangement in which seats are in rows facing the stage area, no tables.

Theme party — a party in which a unique theme is carried through the decorations, food selection, etc.

Time lines — a schedule of each task to be accomplished and who is responsible for it; the core of the program plan.

Tip—a cash award given voluntarily at the time of service as a reward for superior personal service.

Total business value—the sum of all revenue that a meeting will bring to the facility.

Total room nights—the sum of rooms occupied over a specified time frame.

Trade publications—magazines that are produced by professional organizations and are an important source of industry news and education.

Traffic flow—the pattern of the way people move through an area.

Twin room—a room for two people with two beds (single or double).

Value-added tax (VAT)—an incremental fee levied on goods and services; usually expressed as a percentage.

Variable expense—an expense item that changes according to the number of attendees.

Venue—the location of a function.

Very important person (VIP)—a person who has a special function at the meeting (speaker, dignitary, etc.) and who should be treated with special care.

Video conference—video monitors connected by telephone wires, satellite technology, or ground wires to allow individuals to meet "face-to-face" from almost anywhere in the world; a video conference can also include graphics, video clips, and transmission of data or documents.

Walking guest—a guest with hotel reservations who is denied a room due to the hotel's overbooking.

Webcasting—the process of delivering content (words, pictures, audio, and visual) via the Internet.

Well brand—the lowest priced brand of alcohol.

Zone fares—unpublished rates offered from areas of the U.S. and Canada to specified meeting destinations; they do not require Saturday night stay over.

This glossary has been adapted and reprinted with permission from the Professional Convention Management Association (PCMA). For the complete glossary, visit the PCMA's Web site at www.pcma.org, click on Industry Toolbox, and go to "Glossary of Meeting Terms."

Index

A

action plans, 16
ADA, 102
advertising, 58
agenda, daily, 109
agreements, written, 32
associations, for finding speakers, 67
attendees,
    communicating with, 99-112
    travel arrangements for, 105-106
audiovisual department, 85
audiovisual rules, 89-90
authors, as speakers, 67
awards banquets, 143

B

bands, 123-124
banquet department, 85
BEOs, 155, 161

bids, 32
booking process, the, 45-49
breakeven analysis, 25-26
brochure, 99-102
budget sheet, 26
budget, 15
    creating, 23-27
    managing, 32-37
    on-site, 34-35

C

calls, to speakers, 77
caterers, 118-119
catering department, 84
colleges, 43
conference center, 42
contracts, 130-140
    speaker, 140
    supplier, 140
    venue, 130-140
convention centers, 43
copyright, 76

corporate offices, 44
costs, facilities, 29-30
CSM, them 84
CVBs, 40

D

delegating, 21
design, 61-62
destination, 15
details,
    giving a deadline to, 9
    managing, 21
direct mail, 52-55
DMCs, 14

E

e-mail blasts, 55
evaluations, 149-151
    program, 150
    speaker, 149
exhibitors, 145-146

F

facilities, types of, 42-44
facility, working with the,
    83-98
fax blasts, 56
florists, 123
food and beverage, 90-93

G

gratuities, 162-164

H

head counts, estimating, 30
home-base contact, 153
housing, 118

I

insurance, 129
international meetings, 152

L

letter of agreement, 47-48

M

mailing lists, 31, 54-55
marketing, 52-63
meeting bible, 146-147
meeting format, 12
meeting guide, 147
meeting methods,
    alternative, 48-49
meeting purpose, 10
meeting theme, 11
meetings, international, 152
music licensing, 140-141

O

objectives, types of, 10
opening day, 159-164

P

photographers, 124-126
post-meeting, 164-165

pre-con meeting, 154-156
preparation, on-site, 154-159
printing, options for, 62
program evaluation, 150
program guides, on-site., 146-147
program planning, 10
program wrap-up, 111
promotions, 31-32, 51-63
public relations, 56-57

R

registration confirmation of, 103-105
registration desk, 110, 160
registration packets, 106
registration, 115-117
    advance, 115-116
    on-site, 117
reservations department, 86
RFPs, 47
room setups, 93-94, 160-161

S

sales offices, national, 40-41
scripts, 144
security, 120-121
shipping, 162
site inspection, 45-47
site selection, 39-49
    sources for, 39-42
speaker bureaus, 65-66
speaker evaluations, 149

speaker expenses, control ling, 30-31
Speaker Information Form, 76
speakers, 65-81
    communicating with, 71-77
    finding, 65-68
    hiring, 68-70
    selecting, 15
sponsors, 145
stress, 21

T

teamwork, 33
telemarketing, 58
temporary help, 121
thank you notes, 162-164
timelines, 16
to do lists, 16
training centers, 44
transportation, 119-120

U

universities, 43

V

vendors, working with, 113-127
VIPs, 148

W

writing, promotional, 61